History of
INDIAN ARTS
EDUCATION
in Santa Fe

The Institute of American Indian Arts With Historical Background 1890 to 1962

Winona Garmhausen, Ph.D.

Sunstone Press
Santa Fe, New Mexico

FOR: *Jacque*
Jeffrey
Jan
Jill

Cover photographs:
Mescalero Apache Indians from Geronimo's Tribe, arriving at the
 Ramona Indian School, ca. 1890.
U.S. Indian School classroom, 1904
The Seal, Institute of American Indian Arts

First Edition

Printed in the United States of America

Library of Congress Cataloging in Publication Data:

Garmhausen, Winona, 1930-
 History of Indian arts education in Santa Fe.

 Bibliography: p.
 Includes index.
 1. Institute of American Indian Arts--History.
2. Indians of North America--New Mexico--Santa Fe--
Education. 3. Indians of North America--Southwest,
New--Education. I. Title.
E97.6.I57G37   1987   704'.0397   87-18063
ISBN: 0-86534-118-4

Published in 1988 by SUNSTONE PRESS
 Post Office Box 2321
 Santa Fe, NM 87504-2321 / USA

CONTENTS

I
THE UNITED STATES INDIAN INDUSTRIAL SCHOOL AT SANTA FE, 1890-1932

"We must either fight Indians, feed them, or educate them. To fight them is cruel, to feed them is wasteful, while to educate them is humane, economic and Christian."[1]

Commissioner of Indian Affairs
Thomas Jefferson Morgan (1889-93)

Edward Everett Dale states in his book, *The Indians of the Southwest*, that "For three quarters of a century after the adoption of the Constitution there were virtually no Indian schools supported and administered by the government of the United States, and even a hundred years after that event, the program of the federal government for the schooling of American Indian children had only begun."[2] As early as 1819 the United States Congress appropriated $10,000.00 to be used annually for the industrial and scholastic education of Indians (Act of March 3, 1819), but since no mechanism had been established in the Congress to administer these funds, the money was distributed among various missionary organizations to be used in their educational work. Funds which later became available through treaty provisions were also turned over to missionary organizations. These schools, on and off reservations, were called Contract schools. The missionaries in their church schools followed a philosophy of converting and civilizing the "Red Man," and teaching him the white man's language and ways. Until most of the lands of the American Southwest came into the possession of the United States, Indian education was almost entirely carried on by missionary groups. Contract schools were phased out between 1879 and 1901 as public protest against federal aid to sectarian schools, and the constitutional nature of the practice, led the government to discontinue such practices. A system of federally appointed schools resulted, under the jurisdiction of the Bureau of Indian Affairs (BIA).

The Bureau of Indian Affairs had been established in 1824 as part of the War Department, but in 1849 it was shifted to the newly established Department of the Interior. This Bureau, placed in the Department of Interior largely because of problems of Indian land management, became responsible for Indian education. In 1871,

Congressional action prohibited further treaties with Indian tribes. Indians were now confined to reservations and were to be fed, housed, clothed, and protected until such time as Congress considered they were able to care for themselves. The Bureau reports in the years following called for "humanizing, Christianizing, and educating the Indians."[3]

Agents in the Indian field service who worked with the various tribes of the Southwest and who could observe firsthand the conditions under which the Indians lived continued to point out to the federal authorities the need for schools in this region. A philosophy commonly voiced among Indian agents was, "If the Indian was to be advanced, it must be through education at an early age and continued persistently for many years."[4] However, the federal government was slow to establish Indian schools in the Southwest; almost no educational work was done prior to 1870 by the federal government and very little between 1870 and 1880. "The treaties of 1868 with the Navajos and Utes each contained a provision that the Indian would induce all children from seven to eighteen years of age to attend school and that the United States would provide schools for every thirty children of these tribes."[5]

As a result of this commitment by the federal government, the first Navajo day school was established in 1869 at Fort Defiance. In 1878 the Indian agent of the Fort Defiance area reported that, "Thousands of dollars had been spent on transient teachers and even more transient scholars and not a solitary Navajo can either read or write."[6] In this same year there were only six day schools in operation on the reservations of the Southwest. Even though those day schools, established in the sedentary reservation communities, proved to be more successful than those established in the lands of the Navajo where the pastoral pattern of Navajo society caused the children to be constantly on the move, the officials of the Indian service concluded that the day schools contributed little to the education of Indian children. The Indian agents recommended that the day schools be replaced by boarding schools and urged that vocational education be provided for Indian children. The Indian agents may have been encouraged to recommend vocational training for the reservation Indians as it had proved to be successful in bringing Blacks into the mainstream of American society in the East and South. The Blacks who had been denied academic training were beginning to take their place in American industry and farming, based on vocational training provided to them by the Freedman Bureau which was established at the close of the Civil War. However, there were few industrial schools in the United States at this time that could provide such training.

Dale cites the beginning of industrial training for Indian students and the consequences of that training for students of the Southwest:

> In 1878 the federal government made a contract with the Hampton Institute [Virginia] by which that school was to receive and train Indian students, and that year a considerable number were enrolled. Very few of these were from the Southwest, but the opening of Hampton to Indians furnished a precedent for the establishment of new Indian boarding schools of the vocational type at places remote from the homeland of the pupils who attended them. [7]

A major shift in policy came soon after the passage of the Dawes Severalty Act (General Allotment Act of 1887). This act ushered in policies not interrupted until 1934. The Dawes Act had been supported into being by three major groups: 1) those who wished to obtain Indian lands, 2) those wishing the government to withdraw from Indian affairs, and 3) those whose humanitarianism caused them to abhor living conditions on the reservations. The effect of this act was to strip 41 million acres of land from Indian possession. Reservation lands were divided and distributed as individual allotments of 40, 80, or 160 acres to the Indian people, many of whom had traditionally held this land in common. Land declared surplus after distribution to individuals was purchased by the government and resold to provide funds for the education and "civilization" of Indian people. The government had ruled that the Indians would not be permitted to sell their allotment until a period of twenty-five years or longer had passed. Educational policy during this period was designed to fulfill the goals of the Allotment period, a policy which the Commissioner of Indian Affairs said in 1901 would, "if steadfastly adhered to . . . not only relieve the government of an enormous burden, but it is believed will practically settle the Indian question within the space generally allotted to a generation." [8]

Funding for the Santa Fe Indian School, as for all federal boarding schools of the Allotment period, came about as a result of the Dawes Act. The Department of the Interior, acquiring funds generated by this act, began to assume responsibility to a greater degree for Indian education and provided the first really significant funding for Indian schools.

Schools such as Santa Fe's were expected to quickly break tribal ties and dislocate the Indian from his reservation concept.

Skills that he would be given in academic and manual labor training would enable him to effectively manage his own small allotment as an individual farmer or would enable him to live as a laborer off the reservation. He was expected to become a productive American citizen, cognizant of the virtues of daily labor and the power of commanding vocational skills. In fact, the Allotment Act conferred citizenship upon the allotees and other Indians who abandoned their tribes and adopted "the habits of civilized life."[9] In 1890 the Bureau began to subsidize public schools near reservations so as to further break tribal ties. Day schools were encouraged where this was not possible; however, the day schools were frankly seen as feeders for large boarding schools and were usually under the direction of the superintendent of a nearby boarding school. Santa Fe had two such feeder schools in 1890, one at Tesuque Pueblo, the other at Nambe.

It was felt that as long as the Indians lived in their traditional tribal villages, they would retain their "old injurious habits" such as "frequent feasts, heathen ceremonies, dances, and constant visiting."[10]

By 1892 the Commissioner of Indian Affairs was authorized to enforce regulations to secure school attendance of Indian children of suitable age and health. This authority was strengthened the following year by two separate provisions of one act. These provisions authorized the Secretary of the Interior to withhold rations from parents who did not send their children to school.

Fuchs and Havinghurst in their book, *To Live on this Earth*, contend that federal educational policy did not succeed in destroying Indian identity in the reservation and boarding schools because so little schooling was available to Indians at the turn of the century. There were sixteen thousand students in thirteen schools, ages five to twenty-one in 1901. There was also a strong resistance by Indians to this kind of forced assimiliation by education. Fuchs and Havinghurst cite a report by the Commissioner of Indian Affairs in 1901:

Gathered from cabin, the wickiup, and the tents. Partly by cajolery and partly by threats; partly by bribery and partly by force, they are induced to leave their kindred to enter these schools and take upon themselves the outward semblance of civilized life.[11]

Such force was felt to be necessary in the case of the boarding schools as they were supported by the Indian Bureau on annual grants for each student who attended and could be accounted for. A school could not operate unless it could enroll and retain a reasonably large number of pupils. As a consequence, officials made every effort to enroll their schools to capacity and many over enrolled their facilities as much as twenty per cent. (The annual payment per child averaged $167.50 for many years, with gradual increases to $250.00 per year in 1928.)

The Indian boarding school student was cut off from his home, his family, his culture, his early activities and accomplishments, and set down in a white man's world; forbidden to speak his own language, to engage in his arts, crafts, dances, costume, in some cases even to leave the school community. His diet, his dress, his hair style, his shelter, and his activities were all alien to him. Oftentimes he came unwillingly. Some students were literally kidnapped by Indian agents to fill enrollment quotas. Many Indian families feared that their government supplied rations would be cut off if their children did not attend school. Other families hid their children at first from government agents but relinquished them under continued pressure. For some families it was an economic necessity; they could not provide the basic necessities for their children and saw the school, however undesirable, as a means of clothing and feeding their children. Fuchs and Havinghurst comment that:

> Paradoxically, this effort to deal with America's Native population developed in part out of a nineteenth century liberal humanitarianism — an effort to substitute the primer and the plow for the physical extermination which preceded it. [12]

It was directly out of this climate of educational need as perceived by the Bureau officals and commitments by the Congress to administer to these needs that the Santa Fe Industrial School came into being.

The United States Indian School at Santa Fe had its beginnings in the first University of New Mexico, which was founded in Santa Fe by Reverend Horatio Oliver Ladd, a Congregationalist minister. Reverend Ladd had come to Santa Fe from a post as pastor of a Congregationalist church in Hopkinton, Massachusetts. He received an A.M. degree from Bowdoin in 1862 and studied the following year at Yale Divinity School. His original purpose in coming to Santa Fe was to become the principal of the Santa Fe Academy, which was established in 1878 by the New West Education Commission. He arrived in Santa Fe with his wife and son on September 10, 1880.

Ladd's experience with the Santa Fe Academy was not a happy one from the first due to personal difficulties arising from having to adapt to a new and strange environment and the almost immediate friction between him and his board over student discipline and religious instruction. With the financial aid of William B. Berger of Santa Fe and the backing of the New West Education Commission,

Ladd incorporated the University of New Mexico in May, 1881.

In the years that followed, Ladd's interest in Indians and Indian education grew through frequent visits to the pueblos and reservations, and he became known as an Indian reformer. In response to a dramatic plea by San Juan, chief of the Mescalero Apaches, Reverend Ladd established a division of the University devoted to educating young Indian children. Reverend Ladd recalled with some emotion the speech that Chief San Juan made at the Tertio-Millenial exposition held in Santa Fe in 1883. "San Juan with the help of an interpreter described the helplessness of his people to compete with the white man, and especially pleaded for the same education to be given to the Apache children which the white boys and girls received, who would control the future of New Mexico. I was greatly moved by his plea and promised myself that he [San Juan] should have a school in connection with the institution I was building up in Santa Fe."[13] By February of 1884, Ladd's proposal to establish an Indian school at Santa Fe had received the approval of General Whittlesy, Secretary of the Board of Indian Commissioners in Washington, D.C., and that of General Charles Howard, inspector of Indian schools. Letters were sent to Ladd from various members of the Department of the Interior and the Indian Bureau supporting such a concept in Santa Fe. Taking his cue from this official interest, Ladd petitioned Congress for finanacial aid through a House Bill written by E. John Ellis of Louisiana and supported by Representative Anthony Joseph of New Mexico.

After an easy passage in the House and a lengthy and partisan discussion in the Senate led by Senator Dawes, the bill was passed in late 1885, and the University received a $25,000.00 grant and contract scholarships from the Indian Bureau. Each scholarship provided for a grant of $120.00 a year per student to cover all expenses of education, room, and board, for as many Indian students as the University could adequately serve. Ladd sought and received funds for facilities and equipment from the American Missionary Association of New York, eastern philanthropists and church groups, citizens of New Mexico and area states, and the Santa Fe Board of Trade. Citizens of the city of Santa Fe donated a hundred acre tract for the future campus. It was Ladd's practice to take potential contributors and supporters who visited Santa Fe to the nearby pueblos to convince them of the need for an Indian school in Santa Fe.

The Indian Industrial School department of the University was opened on the banks of the Santa Fe River in three adobe dwellings leased from J.E. Taylor on April 1, 1885. During its first year forty-four Pueblo and Apache boys and girls attended classes there and lived in separate housing. The school's population grew quite quickly, and after two years the Pueblo children were assigned by the Roman Catholic Church to St. Catherine's, a new boarding school in Santa Fe, established by Sister Katherine Drexell. The United States Superintendent of Indian Affairs assigned the Mescalero, Jicarilla, and Navajo students to the care of the University authorities. The sudden growth of the University Indian Industrial School population, plus the support of the community and the Bureau, determined the need for industrial training and led the officials of the Bureau of Indian Affairs to decide to establish a distinct industrial school at Santa Fe, entirely supported and governed by the Department of Interior.

Ladd's school continued under the direction of Elmore Chase until 1899. The school was then operated under the auspices of the American Missionary Association as the Ramona Indian School for Girls (re-named for Helen Hunt's romantic heroine, Ramona, from *Ramona*, a popular novel published in Boston in 1884), which had as its goal serving the educational needs of young Apache girls. In 1899 the girls at the Ramona school were transferred to the United States Indian Industrial school which had been built on the site originally intended for Ladd's school.

Reverend Ladd and his wife Lillian, along with teacher assistants, built the primary curriculum at the school on the current modes of boarding school instruction. In addition to training in reading and writing English, as required by the BIA, the students were given manual tasks each day in the kitchens, gardens, carpentry and masonry shops. For the youngest children, the Ladds instituted a kindergarten program. As was the custom in all contract schools operated by religious groups, the students spent part of the day in religious instruction and hymn singing. Public exhibits of the students' work, including handwriting and drawing, were held on a regular basis. The subject matter of these drawings was not recorded in news stories of the time and it is unlikely that they were of a tribal nature as "most missionary groups considered the art expressions of the Indians as heathen" and not to be enouraged. [14]

The students at the University Indian School ranged from the ages of five to twenty-five and came primarily from the northern New Mexico pueblos and Apache communities. The parents of the students were encouraged to visit their children, and it was not uncommon for a Pueblo parent to walk forty miles to the school. Apache parents would travel on horseback two or three times a year, some as far away as 180 miles, to see that their children were properly instructed and cared for.

It is apparent that, although Ladd's purpose paralleled those of other religious reformers, that of civilizing the "Red Man" and gaining converts, he did so with a sense of humanity and with a genuine wish to serve the educational needs of the Indians of the Southwest. New Mexico historian Frank D. Reeve says that, "He furthered the cause of the Indians in their adaptation to the ways of the white man."

The United States Indian Industrial School at Santa Fe, New Mexico was opened to the University students and to all Indian students of the Southwest in 1890. The city of Santa Fe at that time had a population of 8,900 and had become, through the efforts of the Territorial Bureau of Immigration and the Chamber of Commerce, the center of commerce, education, and culture for all of the Territory.

The newly formed Indian Industrial School at Santa Fe was part of the federal boarding school system. This system of education was necessitated partially by the distances and terrain of the reservations, but had as its main purpose the training of young Indian men and women to manage effectively the Allotment lands they had received through the Dawes Act. It was further intended that the training they received would prepare the students to become contributing members of the American society on the farms or in the cities.

The first Superintendent of the United States Indian Industrial School at Santa Fe was S.M. Cart, who remained in charge three years. Of Cart and the Santa Fe school, the Superintendent of Indian Education reported in 1891:

> The Santa Fe School . . . It is finely situated on a commanding site two miles from the city, and the buildings are magnificent brick structures. Superintendent Cart has made a good showing of pupils, over 80, I think, for the first year. This, in a territory whose people are exceedingly conservative in educational matters, and where pupils are obtained only with great difficulty, is a great achievement. Superintendent Cart, is one of the most capable, judicious and hard working men in the service.

Cart was followed by ex-Confederate Army Colonel Jones, who in 1894 established the first Normal school for Indians on the United States Indian Industrial School campus. The Normal Department was continued until 1900 under Jones and his successor, Andrew H. Viets. Little was known locally of these two men other than they

12

were Army-trained and assigned by the Bureau to supervise the Santa Fe school. Santa Fe historians during this period concentrated on "home grown" personalities. As a consequence, such outsiders as Washington-assigned bureaucrats gained very little attention unless they were active in local civic affairs as was Superintendent Clinton J. Crandall, who succeeded Viets in 1900.

Crandall was born in Ohio in 1857, was educated in the "common" schools of Minnesota, and took his higher education at the Normal School of Valparaiso, Indiana. In 1891 he accepted his first school position with the Bureau of Indian Affairs as superintendent of the Indian school at Pipestone, Minnesota. In the years between 1894 and 1900 he was an Indian school administrator and teacher at Chilocco, Oklahoma; at Sacaton in Arizona; and at the Brule Indian School in South Dakota. Based on his experience as a Bureau teacher and administrator, Crandall made the decision soon after his arrival in Santa Fe that the elementary curriculum and industrial training for elementary students would be the school's priorities, as they were in other large federal boarding schools.

The prototype for the Indian Industrial School at Santa Fe was the Carlisle Indian School in Carlisle, Pennsylvania. Carlisle was established in 1879 and continued in operation until 1918. The Carlisle Indian School was founded by Captain R.H. Pratt. Pratt had for three years been in charge of a large group of Cheyennes and Kiowas held as prisoners at Fort Marion, Florida. His management of these Indians won him widespread recognition. With the aid of his wife and a group of ladies of Saint Augustine, he established and conducted a prison school which was so successful that in 1878, when their three year prison sentence had expired, a number of young Indians expressed the wish to remain in the East and secure further education. It was principally to accommodate Pratt's group of students that Hampton Institute, an all-Black school, first opened its doors to Indians seeking vocation training.

The Secretaries of the War and Interior Departments were so impressed with Pratt's work that they aided him in securing the old military post at Carlisle for use as an Indian school, thereby setting the precedent for many Indian schools which would be built on old army bases. In appropriating funds for Carlisle, the War Department enacted a provision that henceforth no officer above the rank of captain should be detailed for Indian education. (Santa Fe's Colonel Jones points out that exceptions were made to this rule.)

The school grew from a small enrollment in 1870 to 543 students in 1885, the year the University of New Mexico in Santa Fe opened its Indian department. In that year six of Carlisle's students were Navajo and ninety-two Pueblo. By the turn of the century Carlisle's enrollment had jumped to well over 1,000 students and continued to be, until its closing in 1918, the most important school in the entire Indian service.

Carlisle's importance to Indian education in the Southwest was not so much due to the numbers of Indian students from the Southwest who attended Carlisle, as their numbers did not at any time comprise a large percentage of Carlisle's population, but because Carlisle became the educational model for all the other large Indian boarding schools which were established in the fifteen-year period after it was founded. The influence of Carlisle's director, Pratt, on the Bureau of Indian Affairs, cannot be understated. Dale comments that:

> Pratt had very definite ideas about Indian education and strove with remarkable energy and ability to put them into execution. He believed that large boarding schools should be established — preferably as remote as possible from the homeland of its students — to which Indian children should be brought and kept a number of years. During this time they were not to return to the reservation or have any personal contact with their families or friends residing on it [the reservation]. He felt that it was far better to take the Indian to civilization than attempt to carry civilization to the Indian. Consequently, he developed a slogan: "To civilize the Indian, put him in the midst of civilization. To keep him civilized, keep him there."[15]

Many of Pratt's innovations were highly praised by Indian Commissioner Leupp and other Bureau officials and became the prevailing methods used in operating boarding schools. Pratt had originated the "outing system," which was used at Santa Fe by Crandall and his successors. Under this plan students were placed with white families during summer vacations, instead of being allowed to return to their reservations. The Indian children lived and worked in these white homes, usually at farm work or domestic service, thereby earning wages and at the same time learning skills which the school superintendents thought would benefit them when they managed their own homes and farms. The students usually returned to the Indian school at the end of the summer with a small sum of money for personal expenses. In some cases students remained with the white family and attended public school, doing sufficient work for the family to pay for room and board.

Pratt and proponents of his "outing system" believed that if the student had no contact with his family and the reservation for several years, he would lose all of his Indian ways of life and become, in everything except the color of his skin, a white man. The flaws in this argument were not apparent to most officials of the Indian Service and most Bureau boarding schools were run on Pratt's tenets for almost half a century. Many school administrators felt that the results of teaching they had accomplished with the student during the nine-month school year would be negated in the three months the student spent at home in the summer. Some day school officals on the reservations declared that the child's home and family undid most of the good accomplished by the school during the six or seven hours a day that the school had control over the pupils.

The Santa Fe Indian School also adopted Carlisle's plan of one half day spent in the academic classroom and one half day spent at manual labor for all its students. The military regimen set up by Pratt and his staff was emulated by all the boarding school personnel of the West and the organization was essentially the same whether the schools were on or off the reservation. All schools were organized on a military basis, with pupils dressed in uniforms and placed in platoons and companies under the command of student officers appointed by the superintendent.

School regulations were enforced, as they were in the public schools of the time, by a demerit system. The student was denied all privileges until the demerits were worked off, usually by additional hours of manual labor. Corporal punishment was used but was probably more common in the public schools of the time. However, most of the larger boarding schools had a "lock up" in which persistent runaways or others who were not affected by ordinary methods of discipline were confined.

Dale describes a typical day at these schools:

Students were roused each morning about six by the bell or notes of a bugle. They dressed quickly and hurried outside to line up under the watchful eyes of their student officers, who conducted the march to breakfast. As soon as it was over, they were marched from the dining room, halted in line and half of them were detailed to work and the other half sent to the school rooms. At noon they marched back to the dining room for lunch, after which those who had worked during the morning were sent to the class rooms and those who had spent the morning hours in school were placed on work detail for the afternoon. School was dismissed around four o'clock and the pupils had an hour and a half or two hours of freedom for play and recreation until dinner, served about five-thirty or six. After dinner there was another hour or more for recreation, but usually pupils had to be in study hall for an hour or two before nine when they returned to the dormitories to make ready for bed. About nine-fifteen taps sounded the warning for lights out, and the Indian student's day ended. [16]

The Santa Fe Indian School was no exception to these rules. A 1916 film in the archives of the State of New Mexico, made as a tourist lure by the Ford Motor Company, shows the students of the Indian School marching in Army-style uniforms and carrying flags about the campus. A strange alikeness was apparent, especially on the boys' faces, which was further intensified by the fact that each boy's thick black hair was cut well above his ears. The rule of the day in the Santa Fe school from 1890 until the middle thirties was cleanliness, discipline, and gruelling hard work. These regulations and military forms were not only severe but were also a hindrance to the formation of any kind of warm relation between teachers and other school employees and pupils.

It was not uncommon during these years to find boarding school students of all ages inadequately nourished and suffering from illnesses for which no medical help or supplies were available. The Santa Fe students, housed as they were in a healthful climate, in sound buildings, in a community that from the first had kept the school under close observation, were a good deal more fortunate than most Indian boarding school students of the same period. However, there were serious illnesses and some students who died were buried on the campus.

From all accounts it would seem that the educational program at the Santa Fe Indian School was typical of most Indian Bureau boarding schools; however, the interest and support shown by the citizens of Santa Fe for "their Indian School" was most unusual. From the beginning the citizens of the city of Santa Fe had supported the concept of an Indian boarding school within its limits through petitions to Congress and gifts of money and land. Over the years Santa Fe supported the Indian school further with many mentions in the local newspapers, frequent visits to the school by dignitaries who had come to the area, and employment provided for the students in the summers and upon graduation. Typical of one of these early newspaper accounts are the following excerpts drawn from a *Santa Fe New Mexican* article written by Superintendent Crandall on August 23, 1904:

> There are now enrolled at the school 431 pupils, representing five tribes . . . out of this number there are at least 350 full-bloods.

> The faculty is composed of teachers, well skilled, who take a deep interest in their work, realizing that to teach Indians requires

perseverance and hard work . . . lower grades are the fullest . . . as few Indians ever go above the eighth grade. They seem to prefer one of the various trades or professions taught. These include: engineering, blacksmithing, tailoring, farming, carpentry, etc. for the boys and dressmaking, cooking and how to become a good housekeeper for the girls . . . Several Indian boys who were in the tailoring department are employed in the Woolen Mills in Albuquerque . . . Forty boys will work in the sugar beet fields in Colorado during the summer. It is difficult to find work for the girls as domestics — housewives don't know how to care for them and they are often led astray.

. . . The boys have just built a cottage on campus . . . . They will be expected to build others next year . . . . We have football, handball and basketball for the boys . . . . The boys make their own shoes and do much of the carpenter work and manual labor about the institution.

It must be taken into consideration that this showing is excellent when it is known that there are a number of obstacles to overcome in order to teach the boys and girls to learn trades and to work. The old Indians object to the young ones learning trades and going out to work as they claim the young Indians will become so acquainted with the white man's customs that they will not come back to the old tribal relations.

From the foregoing it is apparent that Santa Fe's program exemplified the prevailing Bureau philosophy of paternalism and assimilation. The "Red Man" was to be protected, cared for, and given the benefits of the white man's ways, so that he might easily and gratefully become a member of the mainstream of American life. The Bureau government gave neither the student, the student's parents, nor the student's tribal government, any opportunity for assessing the student's needs or requesting educational programming that would fulfill those needs. The missionary spirit of the nineteenth century persisted through new and secular methods.

This view was inadvertently verified by a reporter for *Ranch and Range* magazine who paid a visit to the school in 1901. In an article written for his publication he commented that the Indian students "make their own clothes, shoes, and are taught to depend on themselves and [they are] inspired with an ambition to forsake their old free and easy way of living and adopt civilized ways; to scorn the idea of simply existing but to enjoy the fullness of life." To further support his view, he noted that, "Instead of the sullen obstinate look usually ascribed to the Indian one sees, [there] are on all sides, bright cheerful faces."[17]

No mention can be found in accounts of those early years

at the School of students being allowed or encouraged to engage in their own music, dance, costume, or arts and crafts. *Ranch and Range* magazine makes one small mention of the students playing an Indian game called "Shinney" as part of their physical education program. The Indian student assumed the white man's language, dress, hair style, food preferences, and cultural mores. Those who could not, or would not, became the boarding schools' discipline problem students or frequent runaways.

Crandall, as Viets, Jones, and Cart before him, adhered strictly to the Pratt model at Carlisle, yet they seemed untouched by Carlisle's inclusion of the arts in its curriculum. However, Carlisle and those few government schools which included arts in their curriculum did so in a strictly European context and with a commercial interest. (At Carlisle, English drama was acted out by students dressed as "Indians" in parts in a Pilgrim story.) After 1900 a European-styled art department was established at Carlisle under the direction of an Eastern-trained Indian woman, Angel De Cara-Dietz. One of the stated purposes of the department was to "train and develop the decorative instinct of the Indians to modern methods and to apply it on up-to-date furnishings." Mrs. Dietz, a Winnebago, was assisted by her husband William, a Sioux, who had a similar background. Together they illustrated the school's monthly newsletter and other publications and ran a crafts store at the school for the "traditional" arts of the older reservation Indians. The school sold these traditional crafts — pottery, jewelry, rugs — through a successful mail order business. The students were given training in designing "modern" advertisements for the store sales in the school magazine. In addition to the commercial arts, Carlisle also maintained its own print shop and photography studio.

As early as 1901 the Superintendent of Indian Education regularly covered suggestions for "Native Industries" in his report. These suggestions usually concerned the production of rugs and baskets relating in techniques to the students' tribal backgrounds and were accomplished in the vocational schools as training toward producing saleable items. Hampton Institute and various other federally supported schools did undertake such projects during the early years of the twentieth century. Various superintendents of Indian education urged that only the finest materials be used and that whenever possible the reeds, grasses, and wools be produced at the vocational schools.

Superintendent Crandall and his successor H.F. Coggeshall (1912) and Frederick Snyder (1913) could not have been unaware of such programming during their eighteen years of administration at Santa Fe. For whatever reasons they chose, the "Native Industries" were not developed at the school, nor any European model of arts training. If any drawing was done, it was done as a preparation for vocational projects or as a recreational or extra-curricular activity.

B.J. Bryant, in his discussion of the arts in Bureau of Indian Affairs schools, comments that:

> It should be remembered, however, that the absence of art teaching was common to most schools during this period. The newly established nation needed "useful" vocations in order to provide for its needs, and there was little market for a great deal of artistic production, Indian or otherwise, that did not satisfy one of those practical needs. Art in the civilized world had been long been removed as an activity or expression of the people in the primitive sense, and was practiced largely by specialists. [18]

Bryant further says:

> It is amazing that some of the (BIA) schools encouraged arts and crafts at all, for explicit to the total educational goals was the ultimate eradication of the Indian culture. If anything was accomplished to advance that goal, it was to confuse the Indian student as to the purpose of arts in its traditional sense, and to separate it into a white-oriented pattern. [19]

Crandall and his successors had the complete backing of the Bureau, and the influential Indian policy reformers who gathered annually as "the friends of the Indian" at Lake Mohonk, N.Y., in any additions or ommissions they might make in curriculum which would lead to the assimilation and acculturation of the students placed in their charge. Reformers interested in Indian affairs met each year from 1883 to 1916 at Lake Mohonk, New York to discuss Indian matters and make recommendations. These Lake Mohonk Conferences of Friends of the Indian had tremendous impact on the formulation of federal policy. Commissioner Thomas J. Morgan, in a presentation to the Lake Mohonk Conference in 1889, spelled out a detailed plan for a national system of Indian schools modeled after the public school system. The purpose of this educational reorganization in the Bureau was the final and total Americanization of the Indian through public educational methodology. Noted historian of Indian-white relations, Father Francis Prucha, states that, "Morgan's paternalistic and religious zeal was mixed with an early nineteenth-century humanism and a genuine belief that total assimilation was the true means of happiness for all Indians. [20]

Morgan firmly believed that any educational system was only as good as the civil servants who had been given the charge to carry out the system, and placed great emphasis on the integrity, intelligence, and dedication of those in charge of Bureau education.

As a consequence of Morgan's policies, the Santa Fe Indian School's curriculum in the period 1890 to 1920 closely paralleled the curriculum administered to non-Indian children throughout the country. Its foundation was built on literacy training subordinated to industrial training for those thought less academically inclined, and post-graduate training for only the exceptional student or teachers-in-training. Crandall's philosophy of education and his orientation to student needs, seemingly untouched by his years in the Indian service, came directly out of the industrial revolution of the Midwest. (Had he and other Bureau officials been able to see as Edgar L. Hewett, noted Southwestern anthropologist, saw in 1930, that the "Indian industrial arts" were the making of pottery, baskets, jewelry, the weaving of blankets, leather, beadwork, and costuming, he might have attempted to act upon the students' cultural needs in the School's curriculum.[21]

Morgan's recommended course of study could have led Bureau teachers to include some of the arts in their curriculum, as teachers were enouraged to have the students relate to the legends and stories of their tribes through "oral and written reproduction." Whether or not Santa Fe's teachers followed Morgan's curriculum guides is not known. Many of these teachers were ill-trained, all were poorly paid, and most followed their own preferences in the classroom.

Crandall and his predecessors' views of the Indian school's curriculum based on trends in public school education were legitimate. Manual training had emerged as the most important educational factor at the height of the Industrial Revolution. America's fascination with an exhibit of manual training in the schools by a Russian institute at the Centennial Exposition in Philadelphia in 1876 caused the number of schools throughout the country which offered such training to jump dramatically. Public schools which offered technical training tripled in the years 1890 to 1898.

The movement to include drawing in the public school curriculum began in Boston in 1870. This movement was stimulated by the Exposition six years later and brought to the public's attention by a group of Massachusetts manufacturers who made an appeal to the legislature in 1869 to direct the State Board of Education (the nation's first, founded in 1837) to report some definite plan for introducing schools for drawing or instruction in drawing, free to all men, women, and children in all towns of the Commonwealth of more than 5,000 inhabitants. The industrialists' plea stated that, "Every branch of manufacturing in which the citizens of Massachusetts are engaged requires, in the details of the processes connected with it, some knowledge of drawing and other acts of design on the part of the skilled workmen engaged.[22]

The Massachusetts Board of Education was deeply impressed with the manufacturers' plea and set up a special committee to study the lack of art training in the United States' schools. The committee concluded that America was behind many other nations in supporting art and culture, and because of the lack of training in drawing and design, the very best positions available to artisans and mechanics in America were going to foreign workmen who had come to America with design skills. In 1870 Massachusetts passed a law that drawing would be taught in all public schools for students of all ages, and further required that teachers be trained to instruct in freehand drawing. Massachusetts' cities of over 10,000 persons were required to provide free instruction in industrial or mechanical drawing to persons over fifteen years of age, either in day or night schools. As if to prove its own study, which had concluded the great distances the American schools were behind other countries in art education, the Board employed an Englishman as the nation's first supervisor of drawing in 1870. In 1875, in order to fulfill the legislated needs for teachers of drawing, the Boston Normal Art School was established.

Perhaps it is well that Crandall, his predecessors and immediate successors chose not to introduce weaving and basketmaking as vocational skills. As Bryant has stated, this would have only further confused Indian students by turning what they held as a sacred part of their tradition into a cold and unconnected money-making venture. Classes in drawing taught in the European manner, unrelated to Indian cultures, and incompatible with Indian modes of learning, would have further intensified each student's isolation. (Drawing as a skill was not included in the Bureau's program of study, but was viewed as only an adjunct to mechanical training.) It can only be hoped that the limited sketches these students doubtless had to make in pursuit of their "chosen profession" could be viewed as only a necessary part of learning the white man's skills.

The methods of rote learning, memorization, military discipline, and hard manual labor at the boarding schools, contrasted sharply with the ways by which the Pueblo Indian child was taught.

Carmelita Dunlap, potter of San Ildefonso Pueblo, explains how and why the Pueblo child is taught to make pottery:

> The Indian child learned from imitation. If his mother made pottery, as a small child he played in the dust around her feet as she worked. He ate and drank from pots he saw his mother make. He played in the "mud" with his feet as his mother used her feet to mix the clay. As he grew older he helped to find the clay and the sand, helped to dig it up and bring it home. His eyes often stung from the smoke from the firing pit as he passed the pots to his mother. He experienced his mother's elation at finding a good polishing stone in the riverbed, or just the right piece of yucca for a new paint brush. In time he came to understand the meaning of the designs so lovingly and patiently applied to the pots. One day he would be encouraged to take a lump of "mud" and shape his own pot. Then would come the frustration of not being able to do what his mother could so easily do. But his mother would be patient, she would be kind, she would encourage him and chide him when he was satisfied with less than what was good. If he learned fast and well he would be given special attention by an uncle or aunt or another person of the village and he would in time be able to teach others. His pots would be good, they would hold the food and water and cornmeal for ceremonies. The design would say something special about his people, how they came to be, what they hoped for. He could trade some of these pots for food or other things that were needed in the household to others who could not do as well. He didn't need money, not the way people do now, they would want his pots. [23]

As earlier missionary educators saw the Indian as a possible convert, the Bureau educator saw the Indian as a necessary convert to the white, middle class, dominant culture. The white educator saw himself as a philanthropist willing to share all he held dear with the "nation's poor red savages." [24]

The methods of conversion the white educators employed to reach their assimilationist goals differed very little from other missionary efforts. It was their responsibility as Christian philanthropists to share the religion they held to be true, their language and skills, their love of country, and respect for individualism and private ownership of property. It was not their desire, nor their responsibility as they perceived their role, to study the ways of the Indian groups from which their students came or to adjust their teaching methods to these ways, as this would have been antithetical to their goal of annihilating the old tribal patterns and transforming "lazy savages" into useful citizens.

Because of this indifference to the Indian's culture, very little of worth concerning their teaching and learning methods was recorded by Indian agents and educators who worked on the reservations of the Southwest in the years covered by this study. White anthropologists attempted to fill this void with works of a primary nature in social anthropology in the Pueblos.

Some of what is available to us are studies such as those done by Elsie Clew Parsons. Miss Parsons attempted to study most of the Pueblos of New Mexico during the first half of the century. However, Parsons did not live among the various tribes but stayed in nearby villages where she gathered her information from paid informants — informants whom she did not often trust as she knew that the Indians who cooperated with her were being disloyal to their own tribe.

Such an approach to the study of the culture of a tribal group gives us only an incomplete and outside view, and one that is not particularly helpful in discussing the methods by which Indian elders taught their children and the processes by which their children learned. Unfortunately, many other social anthropologists interested in the Southwest fared little better in their sources or approach to research. Anthropologists such as Ruth Benedict, who were caught up in the theories of social Darwinism, were convinced that these were primitive people whose activities should be observed as being in a lateral progression toward becoming civilized, thereby shutting themselves off from the sophistication of the societies they were attempting to analyze. Even if Parsons and all her contemporaries, had had the extreme good fortune to have been accepted onto the reservations and been shared with openly, freely, and truthfully, they would not have been invited into the most important learning place, the sacred kiva. As a consequence, they would still have had to deal with great gaps in their research.

Harold E. Driver in, *Indians of North America*, reports that Navajo men spend one-third of their time in religious related activities which are kept secret and passed on by word of mouth. The Pueblo Indians are said by Driver to be "more wrapped up in religious ceremony than any other aspect of life."[25] This sacred knowledge, under the threat of injury or death from the tribe, is forbidden to the white man. As a consequence, a total picture of what is taught among the Indians of the Southwest and the process by which it is learned rests in the hands of present and future Indian educators, anthropologists, historians, and others.

Parsons, when faced with the closed society of the Taos Pueblo, found herself reluctantly admiring such conviction and dedicated her study of 1936 to one of these private persons in the following statement:

> To my best friend in Taos, the most scrupulous Pueblo Indian of my acquaintance, who told me nothing about the Pueblo and who never will tell any white person anything his people would not have him tell, which is nothing.[26]

Faced with cultural annihilation in the nineteenth century, the Indians of the Southwest closed ranks and severely punished anyone thought to be giving cooperation to the whites and the federal government. Tribes were turned against each other over this question. In some cases, as with the Hopi, the tribe divided philosophically and physically based on those who were "friendly" or "hostile" to the whites.[27] Hopi Indian, Don Talayesva, in his autobiography, *Sun Chief*, states that the "fear of (the) whites, especially of what the United States Government could do, was one of the strongest powers that controlled us, and one of our greatest worries.[28]

Children did not often come willingly to the Bureau day schools or boarding schools. To do so would have been a disgrace, as no Indian would willingly abandon his culture for that of the white man. As the white man's schools became more acceptable to the Indian, usually some show of defiance by the students was necessary for them to save face with the tribe. Talayesva says of his entrance to day school:

> In 1899 it was decided that I should go to School. I was willing to try it but I did not want a policeman to come for me and I did not want my shirt taken from my back and burned. So one morning in September I left it off, wrapped myself in a Navajo blanket, the one my grandfather had given me, and went down the mesa barefoot and bare headed.[29]

The Indian parents, however, threatened by federal agents or pressed for provisions, dreaded not only the uncertainty of separation from their children but the inevitability that such a prolonged period of the child's life spent in another culture would do much to alter the child's views towards his tribal ways. As we have seen in remarks by Superintendent Crandall and the reporter of *Ranch and Range* magazine, Bureau officials were aware of the misgivings of the tribal elders and saw these misgivings as a hindrance to furthering their educational programs.

Th elders of the tribes had good reason to fear such changes, for then as now, changes often came to the group through value changes

24

in the children of the group. Helen Sekaquaptewa in her autobiography, *Me and Mine*, relates that many Hopi children returning from long stays in boarding schools could not reconcile themselves to the physical realities of their village homes with dirt floors, no windows, and no indoor sanitary facilities, and they sought to make their parents agree to changes in their home environment before they would return to live on the reservation. Such abrupt changes from tribal traditions, made to accommodate their children, soon put these parents out of step with their neighbors, and bad feelings ensued among tribal members.

It is difficult to perceive the cultural shock experienced by the Indian child taken from his home, or reluctantly sent from his home to a government school many miles away. At this place he was met by bright lights, fences, and military personnel. He was stripped, bathed, his hair cut, called by a new name, given unfamiliar food, and put in a place unlike his home with children from other tribes, where all were spoken to in a foreign tongue.

Incidents from autobiographies told to white writers by Indians who exprienced the government schools are so touching in their descriptions of the loneliness, hunger, confusion, frustration, and heartbreak, that one cannot read them without becoming painfully aware of the contrasts between the child's home and school environment. These accounts sometimes touch on home experiences of the child and give us the only first-hand information we have concerning his early tribal learning experiences.

Of early childhood learning among the Hopi, Helen Sekaquaptewa says:

> Sending children to school was not the Hopi way of education. They had on-the-job training. Children learned to care for the sheep and raise corn in the day-to-day school of experience. Girls learned from their mothers to grind corn, prepare the food, and care for the household. Men and boys met in the kiva in winter time for lessons in history, religion and traditions—all taught in story and song. Here also was learned respect for their elders and for tribal and clan codes.[30]

Sekaquaptewa says further that all Hopi learning had a purpose and she describes this water-carrying ritual as performed by young girls imitating the older women as showing that even a relaxing activity was structured.

> There was a time for big girls to carry water too. This was more of a social affair than a necessity. After the girls had finished grinding [corn] for the day they would form a party and go late in the afternoon. They walked out of the village in single file with their vessels on their

backs. When they were outside the village they could walk in groups visiting with ease. The girls would go to a smaller spring, farther from the village, and might not find nor bring any water back. The idea was for relaxation, but it had to appear that they had a purpose.[31]

Helen, as other Indian children, was talked with frankly about sex from the time she was a small child. At menstruation her mother instructed her in the Hopi moral code. She was made to understand the reason for separation of the sexes which was enforced until marriage. This sort of openness and training was not available to the boarding school student. In fact, school children living in a mixed society were often severely punished by school officials for expressing normal curiosity in sexual matters.

Francis La Flesche, Omaha Indian, recalls from his childhood experiences that:

> Among my earliest recollections are the instructions wherein we were taught respect and courtesy toward our elders; to say "thank you" when receiving a gift, or when returning a borrowed article; to use the proper and conventional term of relationship when speaking to another, and never to address anyone by his personal name; we were also forbidden to pass in front of persons sitting in the tent without first asking permission; and we were strictly enjoined never to stare at visitors, particularly at strangers. To us there seemed to be no end to the things we were obliged to do, and to the things we were to refrain from doing.[32]

La Flesche explains further of early language training that:

> From the earliest years the Omaha child was trained in the grammatical use of his native tongue. No slip was allowed to pass uncorrected, and as a result there was no child-talk such as one obtains among English-speaking children, the only difference between the speech of old and young was in the pronunciation of words which the infant often failed to utter correctly, but this difficulty was soon overcome, and a boy of ten or twelve was apt to speak as good Omaha as a man of mature years.[33]

The Indian child's body was considered sacred by his elders. Because of this one did not physically punish a child lightly as such abuse was thought to injure the child's personality and health. Instead, the Indian child learned acceptable behavior codes because he was rewarded for appropriate performance and was ignored for inappropriate behavior, except in the unusual cases in which the offense was one that traditionally was dealt with in a physical sense. Each task the child was given had a purpose and that purpose related in some way to the survival of the family and tribe. Survival tasks were inextricably bound to ritual and the ritual bound to the religion of the tribe. The child's behavior and task performance were controlled by praise, ridicule, and fear of reprisal from his elders and spirits and spirit groups.

Driver states that:

Indian children probably learned more from free imitation and less by conscious instruction than do children in the modern Western world. Nevertheless, many instances are reported of children being taught both essential tasks and games by parents and other elders. This distinction between work and play was less sharp among Indians than it is in our modern world. [34]

The Hopi Indian, Talayesva, says of his early learning:

Learning to work was like play. We children tagged around with our elders and copied what they did. We followed our fathers to the fields and helped plant and weed. The old men took us on walks and taught us the use of plants and how to collect them. We joined the women in gathering rabbit weed for baskets, and went with them to dig clay for pots. We would taste this clay as the women did to test it. We watched the fields to drive out the birds and rodents, helped to pick peaches to dry in the sun, and gathered melons to lug up the Mesa. We rode the burros to harvest corn, gather fuel, or herd sheep. In house building, we helped a little by bringing up dirt to cover the roofs. In this way we grew up doing things. All the old people said it was disgrace to be idle and that a lazy boy should be whipped. [35]

Talayesva tells further of his learning experiences in a chapter from *Sun Chief* entitled "Learning to Live.' He makes it clear that all of his learning experience was based on basic survival with food, water, and fuel being the focus of all activities. He tells of long hours spent in childhood games and days spent in the kiva listening to the stories and songs of the old men who taught as they wove. His childhood work and games taught him to have a deep respect for plant and animal life. From his family he learned the Hopi rules of hospitality and the legends of his people. He was taught how to hunt, the rudiments of herbal medicine, how to tame a burro, whom to trust, and what he most certainly would be punished for. He says of this time:

By the time I was six . . . I had learned to find my way about the Mesa and avoid graves, shrines, and harmful plants, to size up people, and to watch for witches. [36]

From these brief accounts it is apparent that the education the

Indian child received at home differed greatly from the schooling he received in the government schools. At school, away from his family and tribe, the work he was given to do seemed fragmented and purposeless. He found himself physically punished or isolated for offenses which had no meaning for him. He was often denied adequate food — an experience that from childhood he had been taught to fear most. He must respond to a new nonsensical first name. He was expected to express himself as an individual, instead as a part of a whole, in a sexually and tribally mixed society, areas forbidden to him in the past. Yet he could find himself severely punished for expressing sexual curiosity, an area of concern openly dealt with in his family. He was expected to become competitive, to seek favors for activities alien to him, and to find areas of comfort, cut off from his own religion, arts, food, clothing, shelter, and tribal routines. The contrasts between the old and new lives of these children are staggering. It is not to be wondered at that many students capitulated to their captors' methods of inculturation and learned to dread their trips home and turned for a time against their people. Talayesva states that many times during his boarding school experience he desperately wished "that there were some magic that could change my skin into that of a white man."[37]

There can be no doubt that Bureau educators, until the middle thirties and beyond, closed themselves completely to the notion of education based on cultural differences or skills taught which related to the Indian students' culture. Bureau educators, versed since the middle of the nineteenth century in the goals of paternalism and assimilation, continued to view themselves as paid philanthropists who had a moral obligation to administer to the nation's primitive peoples so as to transform them into self-supporting and loyal citizens, and thereby remove the burden of their care from the American public. No theory of specifically Indian education was sought or incorporated into Bureau policies. This might be expected, since the American public school system, on which the Bureau schools were modeled, was similarly making no effort to tailor its programs to the many ethnic groups it served for much the same purposes. This was the period of "100% Americans" stoking the fires under the great "melting pot," a period of massive immigration that led America to push for the eradication of ethnic differences in the most powerful nation of the world. This was also a period of great building in American industrial strength. The public schools of the nation were slow to add the arts to curriculums, as the arts were thought to contribute little to skills needed to survive in a mechanized society. The Bureau, lagging painfully behind public education, was even more reluctant to provide time and space for a discipline not seen as marketable or amenable to the annihilation of a culture.

It would seem from the following description of the Santa Fe Fiesta parade written by Paul Horgan in the middle twenties that the arts education battle was indeed lost.

> The Indian was not neglected. His dances were offered by selected groups from various Pueblos; and in the Fiesta parade, his teachers at the U.S. Indian School sponsored floats on which young Indians rode, smiling and full of pep, wearing varsity sweaters, and sanctioning in innocent good manners the slogans printed on large placards above them. One, showing a vocational machine shop worked by Indian youths with a white man posed as their teacher, read this way: "Papoose want um be big chief Machinest." Another, showing a young Indian astride a stuffed bucking horse, read: "Me, 'um' enjoy riding Mustang."[38]

Horgan concludes, "In the young Indian's acceptance of his conqueror's comic-strip view of him, the conquest was complete."

However grim this description appears to the reader, it does bring a note of hope. The Pueblo Indians, long under threat of banishment of their dances, were now dancing in public; the Indian students were being encouraged to participate in the Santa Fe Fiesta as a recognized group. Much of this attention and support had come about because of the large number of artists, anthropologists, and writers who discovered the Santa Fe area after the turn of the century. These men and women who had emigrated to the Southwest to avail themselves of the Indian and Spanish cultures became the staunchest supporters of Indians' civil rights, and protectors and disseminators of the Indians' cultural heritage. Horgan explains that, "In the Pueblo Indian the U.S. found its last romance with aboriginal America."[39] This romance was to eventually lead to a resurgence of Indian arts in the Southwest and this movement would vastly affect the lives of Indians in the Southwest and elsewhere.

The Santa Fe Indian School in the years immediately preceding 1920 went on much as it had from Superintendent Crandall's early days. Paying little or no attention to the multitude of linguistic and other cultural differences among Indian people, the Bureau continued on the course it had set for itself in the 1890's. The significant changes in Indian education were taking place outside the boarding schools and would not be felt inside for more than a decade.

Boarding school education during this period stagnated and fell even more seriously behind trends in public school education. High school or specialized training was available to the fortunate few. The industrial training provided at these schools was proving most often useless on the reservation and inadequate to job opportunities in towns and cities.

To further compound problems with the boarding school curriculum, a uniform course of study was imposed on all federal Indian schools in 1916. "The uniform curriculum was planned with the vocational aim very clearly dominant, and with a special emphasis on agriculture. Expressing a concern for relevance related to assimilationist goals, the program states: 'The character and amount of academic work has been determined by its relative value and importance as a means of solution of the program of the farmer, mechanic, and housewife'."[40]

The Bureau banned tribal arts and crafts training in all of its schools until 1930. The dance and music of the Native American was thought such a threat to assimilation that Congress for years, pushed by religious and moralistic forces, found itself on the brink of banning these performing arts altogether, on and off the reservation. Reform of such injustices was to come in many ways and from many persons during those tumultuous years of the twenties. The arts community of Santa Fe would play an especially large part in social reform and in affecting future educational programs for Indian children.

In 1918, Congress passed an act (Act of May 25, 1918, 40 Statute Law 564) which refused full scholarships to children of less than one-fourth Indian blood and designated that these children should attend public schools. This forced a drop in boarding school attendance and reinforced the Bureau policy, in effect since the turn of the century, which encouraged public school and day school attendance on or near the student's home reservation. These changes forced even further economic hardships on the boarding schools, making the student's labor role considerably more significant in the support of his institution. Congress in 1929 repealed a 1908 act that had limited per capita expenditure for boarding school students, but by that time the boarding schools were under severe public attack and investigations by the Senate.

Stirred to action in the early twenties by the prohibition of Indian dances, the arts community of Santa Fe found itself at the center of action which would take the Indians' economic and social plight to the very doorsteps of the American public. Erna Fergusson, in her book, *New Mexico: A Pageant of Three Peoples,* vividly recalls those well-established artists who came to live and work in New Mexico. She mentions such notables as painters Marsden Hartley, Robert Henri, B.J.O. Nordfelt, Russell Cowles, and John Sloan. Of Sloan's various contributions to New Mexico she comments, "Perhaps his wife, Dolly, a sixty-inch dynamo, a vetern of suffrage parades" was his greatest contribution. "Dolly threw herself into the effort to defeat the Bursum Bill to save the Pueblo's lands; she lined up so many New York writers in a cause they had never heard of that New Mexico's Indians became front page stuff and the *Santa Fe New Mexican* was displayed on New York newsstands."[41] The Bursum Bill was the work of Senator Holm O. Bursum of New Mexico who in 1922 introduced a bill to acquire title to lands within the Pueblo land grants. The bill would have given strong advantage to the whites in their disputes over land title with the Pueblos. The bill was passed by the Senate on September 11, 1922, but violent opposition to it by the Indians and their friends led to the ultimate defeat of the bill.

Fergusson comments that writer Mary Austin, who had brought with her from California her mystical preoccupation with "Amerindian culture," took a more militant view as she "pushed for action." "Her (Austin's) followers laughed at her, but they loved her and she led them." From Austin's perch on the bootblack's stand in the Santa Fe Chamber of Commerce, she managed to enlist young men in the physical labor of saving the church at Acoma Pueblo, raised money to purchase and restore the Santuario at Chimayo (which was then presented to the Catholic Church), and gave her blessings to the formation of the Indian Tribal Arts Association, headed by the Sloans and Misses Amelia Elizabeth and Martha R. White. The purpose of the Association was "to hold Indian craftsmen to their highest standards and to educate the public to appreciate the best."[42]

The defeat of the Bursum Bill led to the formation in 1922 of the New Mexico Association on Indian Affairs, led by Mrs. Margretta Dietrich. This organization defended Indians as individuals and tribes and became a lobby to Congress of some strength and importance. Oliver La Farge, noted writer and anthropologist, headed the Association's eastern counterpart, The Association on American Indian Affairs, and lent his skill as a writer with personal knowledge of the Indians of the Southwest, to matters of reform.

Fergusson concludes that, "Indians for the first time met respectful comprehension. After centuries of the white man's scorn, smug superiority, and condescension, their dances were witnessed by quietly attentive people who recognized their artistry and religious content. Their handiwork was judged with artistic discrimination."[43]

Mary Austin explains the beginning of her role in the Indian reform movement in her autobiography, *Earth Horizons:*

> The whole business of affecting the governmental policy toward Indians as the Government is now willing to admit it has been affected, might just as well have been any other of those half-unconscious starts of my generation toward the realization and rescue of the underdog, which has been its characteristic concern. At the same time that my contemporaries were joining labor organizations and aligning themselves with wage-strikes, I took the defense of Indians because they were the most conspicuously defeated and offended against group at hand. I should have done as much even without what I afterward discovered among them of illumination and reformation of my own way of thought.[44]

The preservation of the Indian dances was crucial to the work of an organization called the Indian Arts Fund that the artists had put together in 1924. The dance controversy was used to call public attention to the work that the Fund was doing in collecting notable examples of Indian arts. As Austin wrote, "The Bureau, possessed of the idea that we were corrupting the tribesmen, issued an order that they should be stopped. There was a protest on the part of the artists, opposed by the missionaries and supported by the visitors."[45]

The Indian Arts Fund which was championed by Austin, poet Alice Corbin Henderson, John Sloan, anthropologist Kenneth Chapman, muralist Olive Rush, and other noted persons, had as its purpose the collection of Indian arts of the past so that all "the notable art works should not be carried away by tourists and random collectors." Austin explains that they wanted "an Indian museum for Indians; where they could refresh themselves in the notable examples."

John D. Rockefeller came to Santa Fe for a visit, saw the collection, which was housed in the Museum of New Mexico, and expressed his interest to the Arts Fund group in assisting them in building a museum for the collection. The group informed Rockefeller that they wished the museum "to be a living one, for the benefit of Indians and the pouring of their capacity into the streams of American culture." Rockefeller was delighted with their direction, saying that such a museum had been in his thoughts for some time. As a result, he contributed not only to building the museum but donated a number of art works from his own colleciton to the Indian Arts Fund. The Whites, Austin, and others from the group donated the land for the museum and anthropologist Kenneth Chapman was named curator of the collection.

Kenneth Chapman had by the twenties established himself as an authority and writer on Indian pottery design. He had also become a leading force along with anthropologist Edgar L. Hewett in preserving and collecting Indian art works while working with the School of American Research (SAR), established in 1907 in Santa Fe by the Archaeological Institute of America. Chapman as early as 1901 had independently encouarged young Indians of the Southwest to paint and had provided them with materials so that they might depict their tribal images. Chapman in turn purchased many of these works for his studies.

Edgar L. Hewett, also drawn to Santa Fe as was Chapman by Adolph Bandelier's work in archaeology, had many opportunities while working on the excavations of ancient ruins in the Frijoles Canyon to discover ancient rock pictures, cave paintings, and pottery shards, which led him to encourage the people of the nearby San Ildefonso Pueblo to renew their interest in these art forms.

The story of the beginning of the Indian arts movement at San Ildefonso Pueblo, home of some of the ancient people who centuries before had abandoned their dwellings in Frijoles Canyon, varies with the teller. From all accounts, however it seems that two facts can be counted on: 1) that a grade school teacher in the San Ildefonso day school, as early as 1910, encouraged her students to draw, and 2) that about the same time anthropologists associated with the SAR played an active patronage role. The SAR conducted excavations at Frijoles Canyon from 1904 to 1914. The uncovering of prehistoric mural fragments inspired emulation of the designs on the part of the Indian laborers and Hewett provided them with materials and a ready market for their art. Alfredo Montoya, the first adult San Ildefonso painter, sold pictures to the SAR people at their camp in 1909. Montoya died in 1913.

Hewett encouraged Cresencio Martinez, brother-in-law to Montoya and worker at the camp, to produce pictures of his Pueblo's tribal ceremonies, which Cresencio completed in 1917, a year before his death. Julian Martinez, who married the potter Maria in 1904, is said to have made crayon drawings at San Ildefonso as early as 1908. J.J. Brody states in his book, *Indian Painters and White Patrons,* "Without question, the proto-modern painters of San Ildefonso themselves became the first modern Indian painters."[46]

However confused the facts of its beginnings, a new school of Indian painting quickly grew in San Ildefonso, which is the acknowledged birthplace of modern Indian painting and center for a re-birth in traditional pottery-making. News of the happenings at San Ildefonso travelled quickly throughout the Southwest, and soon day school teachers throughout the area were encouraging their young students in the painting of tribal motif pottery designs, mural painting, and embroidery. The SAR and later the Indian Arts Fund, through Kenneth Chapman, provided drawings and photographs of art of the past to these interested teachers for their students' research. Noted artists of the Pueblos and reservations, such as potter Maria Martinez, were invited into the day school classrooms to demonstrate and instruct the children in their own tribal arts.

Soon other young Indians of the Southwest came forward and expressed their interest in paintings. Among these were: Aiwa Tsireh (Alfonso Roybal) from San Ildefonso; Fred Kabotie, Hopi; Otis Polelonema, Hopi; and Ma pe wi (Velino Shije Herrera) of Zia Pueblo. By 1919 the new Indian painters had gained such attention through their various noted Santa Fe supporters that a well-publicized exhibit of Indian watercolors was held at the Arts Club of Chicago. John Sloan arranged two shows for these young artists in New York in 1920. Over the next few years John Sloan, Alice Corbin Henderson, Chapman, and others would provide national shows on a yearly basis for the emergent artists. The Santa Fe Fiesta Council provided for an Indian Market and the Museum of New Mexico held yearly shows of new paintings. Thus was established what came to be known as the Santa Fe School of Art.

Tsireh, Kabotie, and Herrera, students at the Santa Fe Indian School, were encouraged and permitted by Superintendent and Mrs. John De Huff to paint after school hours at the school. In 1921 the SAR employed these three painters to paint for their collection.

Santa Fe's close proximity to many Indian reservations and the emphasis of the Santa Fe arts organizations on the exhibit and sale of Indian art works soon made Santa Fe a mecca for tourists. As Paul Horgan says, all tourism efforts were forced to bring the tourist "face to face with the leading exhibit of all, which was the Indian." Rail accommodations were plentiful and auto traffic was fast developing. Accommodations along the way at the Fred Harvey chain of hotels, shops, and restaurants, such as the La Fonda in Santa Fe, gave Santa Fe the reputation of being "the place to go" for people of culture and taste, after the turn of the century. The Santa

Fe Fiesta, established as a commercial venture in 1919, the opening of the Museum of New Mexico in 1909, the Fine Arts Museum in 1917, and various other exhibits of Pueblo life, "told the traveler what he presently would see in actuality."[47] In the twenties, early immigrants and tourists became the disseminators nationwide of the Santa Fe Indian Arts movement. And this movement, catching the attention of Indian and non-Indian educators, would not only greatly alter public attitudes toward the Indian, but would influence the entire future of his education.

The stage was set for change. The Congressional mood moved toward reform in Indian matters and the Congressional committees began to investigate Indian education. The American public, greatly excited by its new mobility, had the opportunity to readily grasp some of the problems of the Indians existence for the first time. Educator John Dewey's philosophy of progressivism led to the formation in 1919 of the Progressive Education Association. This education philosophy, which emphasized the relation of learning to the child's interest, would influence the Bureau schools to include the arts in their curriculum.

The Bureau personnel, affected by public opinion and emerging trends in education, began slowly to take a second look at the boarding school programs. The reservation day school teachers, encouraged by the response to their efforts, had taken independent steps toward including the students' tribal arts in their daily programs. These day school teachers and supportive anthropologists had done much to spread the news of the results of these early experiments in national educational journals. All these events led to the development of a new kind of Bureau administrator. Such an administrator was John De Huff, Superintendent of the Santa Fe Indian School from 1918 to 1926.

John De Huff was born, as was Crandall, in Indiana, and received his early education there. He later attended Indiana State University and the University of New Mexico. Prior to coming to the Santa Fe Indian School he spent twelve years in public school work in the Philippines; the last three years of which he spent as Superintendent of Public Instruction in Manila. He resigned his position at the Santa Fe Indian School in 1926 to become the executive secretary of the Santa Fe Chamber of Commerce, a post which he held for twenty years.

De Huff's wife, Elizabeth, was a former teacher, noted writer, and lecturer on Indian lore. Mrs. De Huff was trained at Lucy Cobb Institute in Athens, Georgia; Teacher's College; and Barnard

College in New York. Shortly after her arrival in Santa Fe she began to publish articles, short stories, and plays based on Indian legends.

De Huff, restrained by Bureau policies, carried on his predecessors' curricular footsteps. He did not change the military regimen, split days, or emphasis on industrial and agricultural training in the School's curriculum. But through the influence of the Santa Fe arts reform movement, and doubtless his wife's interest in Native American history, he opened up to the possibility, if not the actuality, of offering arts in the academic curriculum.

We are given a privileged look into De Huff's emerging educational philosophy in a paper he presented in 1922 to a group of Indian service teachers attending a summer session at the Northern Arizona Normal School in Flagstaff, Arizona. The topic of his paper was "How Should We Educate the Indian?". In this paper De Huff anticipates the change in attitude in Bureau education by many years when he states that one of his principal aims is "to foster and preserve the Indians' native culture."[48] Although still somewhat hampered in his thinking by the old tenets of paternalism and assimilation, De Huff laid the groundwork for a new kind of education which fully took into account the Indian's cultural heritage and his tribal differences. De Huff's experiences with young painters at the School, whom he had encouraged since 1918 to work outside the program, had led him, along with other prevailing education influences, to take a strong public stand for the arts in education.

The De Huffs in 1922 put on a play written by Mrs. De Huff and which included Pueblo Indian dances, at the closing of the school year. The Santa Fe Fiesta Board asked that the dances from the play be presented at the Fiesta in September of the same year, at a payment of $200.00 to the dancers. That year also marked the beginning of an "Indian industrial arts and crafts exhibit," to which the Indian school students were encouraged to contribute, which became a regular part of the Fiesta. Although prohibited by Bureau policy to include the "traditional" arts in its regular curriculum, the Santa Fe Indian School had managed through the De Huffs and the support of the arts community to provide opportunities for some of its students to express themselves in the arts a number of years before other off-reservation boarding schools would have such opportunities. The School itself was still devoted to basic literacy training and preparation in the industrial skills on the elementary level. However, as Hewett noted, a new realization of what industrial skills for the Indian could be, was finally on its way.

De Huff cooperated fully with organizing the annual Indian Fair held in connection with the Santa Fe Fiesta, using the school as a collecting place for work that was sent to the shows from the reservations and pueblos. He obtained Bureau approval for this activity and reported in 1926 on the continuing success of the show saying, "Many members of the Bureau school and field service have assisted year after year in collecting and displaying exhibits from their districts and giving information to visitors."

In time those artists who contributed to these shows, such as Maria the potter, and painter Tonita Roybal, would come to be known as the leading figures in Indian art. The interest in the shows generated among artists and writers on Indian crafts and their symbolism caused further pleas to be made for the inclusion of the study of Indian culture in school curriculums. In such an article Alice C. Henderson reasons that, "Again our artists are endowed with scholarships to enable them to study classical or archaic Greek or Roman art in Italy or Greece; but where is the scholarship to send young art students to Arizona or New Mexico to study a living art or design as unique as that of Greek or Etruscan vases?"[49]

The Santa Fe shows also encouraged the use of Indian motifs in the public school programs of the late twenties in the Southwest, as evidenced by a report from the Santa Barbara, California school system carried in the *Albuquerque Morning Journal* which states that, "As a result of the revival of Indian arts and designs begun by the School of American Research almost 20 years ago, many of the public schools of the state are now turning to Indian designs as a fertile field for examples in art instruction."

In 1926 a new superintendent, Chester E. Faris, was appointed at the Santa Fe Indian School. Faris had come from a position as Superintendent of the Northern Pueblos region. He had worked many years for the Bureau with the Jicarilla Apaches in northern New Mexico. Faris had gained a fine reputation with the Bureau in rehabilitating the Jicarillas, who had sunk into desperate poverty as a result of the Allotment Act. Through the leadership of Faris, the Jicarillas learned to develop their divided lands, raise cattle, and halt the malnutrition and disease that had threatened their existence.

Little has been recorded of Faris in these early years except a quote from a magazine article that goes far in explaining his success in his eventual encouraging of the arts at the Indian School. Concerning the simplicity of his method, he said, "I always made a rule never to tell an Indian what to do. I waited until he told *me* what he wanted and then I helped him to get it."[50]

The Indian reform movement raged on throughout the United States in the twenties as it had in Santa Fe. By 1924-25 it had reached a high pitch. The American Defense Association, which had come into existence as a direct result of the Bursum Bill, had managed throughout the twenties to keep problems of Indian education in the public's consciousness. It was led by John Collier whose interest in Indians dated to 1920, when he and his family visited with Mabel Dodge Luhan in Taos. His first interest in the communal life of the Taos Indians led him to a lifelong interest in the Indian's welfare. In 1923, a group of reformers met in Washington as the Committee of One Hundred to discuss the direction of Indian affairs and make suggestions for their improvement. The recommendations of this committee, particularly in the area of education, were noteworthy, but they had little effect on the Bureau. In 1926, again seeking independent opinion, the Department of the Interior, under Hubert Work, commissioned the Brookings Institute to investigate the entire Bureau structure. Dr. Lewis Meriam of the Brookings Institute, assisted by a team of experts, evaluated Indian education for the first time in a comprehensive manner. Their report, "The Problem of Indian Administration," was submitted to Work in February of 1928. The education section of the report was prepared under the direction of W. Carson Ryan Jr., a talented and well-known educator who had worked for the United States Bureau of Education from 1912 to 1920 and was then a professor of education at Swarthmore. Ryan, through his many years of educational experience, had become committed to the new concepts of progressive education.

The boarding schools were hardest hit by the report, although all aspects of Indian education had been evaluated. Overcrowding, the use of child labor, malnutrition, illness, poorly prepared personnel, inadequate funding, the evils of the standardized curriculum based on white cultural values, and military regimen and discipline were openly deplored in the report.

Reformers pressed for the closing of the boarding schools, but Ryan felt rather than closure, operational change was in order. He strongly recommended, however, that reservation community day schools and public schools near the reservation be used whenever possible, and that boarding school attendance be reserved for the older student and the adult.

The Meriam Report opened the door to the introduction of traditional Indian arts in the boarding school curriculum. Ryan recommended that the "Native Arts and Industries" be encouraged. He urged the hiring of personnel to supervise the production and marketing of native crafts in the industrial boarding schools. He also suggested that such a program might be extended to the reservations to create industries there under government control and supervision. Most importantly, Ryan recognized the importance of the arts in the new curriculum, where they might lend themselves to curriculum building, "based on the ascertained needs of Indian boys and girls and adapted to their aptitudes."

For the first forty years of its existence on the U.S. Indian Industrial School at Santa Fe served elementary school children only, graduating its first high school class in 1934. In fact, until 1928, there were only six schools in the Bureau system that had full high school programs. At various times, as mentioned above, there were post-graduate teacher programs and post-elementary technical training offered at the School. These programs were dependent for their existence on the educational mood of the Indian Bureau and the curricular preferences of the area directors.

The recommendations of the Meriam Report were implemented in most cases by area directors, as these administrators still retained much of their power and autonomy in the years directly following the Report's publication. The Santa Fe Indian School students were especially favored by the new funding procedures and the curricular preferences of Superintendent De Huff and Chester Faris, his successor. Within three years a secondary education program was established at the School and an arts and crafts building was on its way to completion.

Dorothy Dunn, in *American Indian Painting*, contends that the "logical place for the government to begin encouragement of the arts was in the Indian schools and that Santa Fe was the place to start."

From the Meriam Report in 1928, however, until 1931 when the new arts and crafts building was opened, the boarding school routine, established forty years before at Santa Fe, continued on much as it had begun. Brody says, "The Santa Fe Indian School was a restrictive institution, more reminiscent of a prison than a modern day school."[51]

The results of years of this kind of training were to lead H.J. Hagerman, Special Committee of the U.S. Indian Service, to comment in Santa Fe in 1931:

> It is a serious question as to what has been so far the actual result of our education on the younger generations of Indians [of the Southwest] . . . . The younger generation of educated Indians — the quantitative turnout of our schools — are so far a rather uncertain product.[52]

Perhaps Hagerman hit upon the reason for such dubious educational results from the Bureau's point of view when he commented in a later chapter of his report on *Native Culture and Amalgamation* that: "Assimilation so far in the Southwest has not been very extensive or successful, in spite of the sincere efforts of the Indian Office through placement officers, matrons and others to make it so." He admitted that the Navajos especially "are enormously entertained by our manners, clothes and customs." And he concluded that, "One must always remember that there are still quite a lot of people in the United States of America, descendents of those who were here long before any of us, who still look upon us as queer birds whose main characteristics are pomposity and bluff."

II
THE SANTA FE INDIAN SCHOOL
1930-1962

Within the last fifteen years, a very definite movement has been growing and is still growing, to try to restore this lost tradition [art] to the Indian. We cannot restore the lands we have taken from him: it is not within our civilization to do so. But we can restore to him his art tradition, awaken his pride in his own achievement, stimulate his native creative instinct, until he carries on again, producing as beautiful and lovely creations as he did before.[1]

Margaret McKittrick, Field Investigator, Eastern New Mexico
Association on Indian Affairs.

A great deal of myth surrounds the formation of the painting studio at the Santa Fe Indian School (SFIS) in 1932; a myth that the first fine arts instructor to be allowed in a BIA school was allowed here, that students hadn't been permitted previously to produce or exhibit their tribal designs in a school or outside setting, a myth that the tribal arts hadn't been integrated into academic curricula by qualified instructors, and a further myth that no murals on public building walls had been done by Indian students previous to those supervised by noted Southwestern muralist Olive Rush at the SFIS in 1931.

Although Dorothy Dunn, who began and supervised the studio at the SFIS from 1932 to 1937, has written prolifically of her studio experience, both during and after her tenure there, her writings tend to minimize those arts activities which took place in BIA day schools throughout the country, in other boarding schools such as Haskell Institute, Carlisle, and the Albuquerque Indian School, prior to 1932. This is explainable, perhaps, when one views the near hysteria focused by Santa Fe artists, anthropologists, Indian arts organizations, and Indian reform groups who were working for the preservation and renewed production of "traditional" Indian art forms in the Southwest. These attentions had been focused on the SFIS as the center of and catalyst for such activity by these individuals and groups since the De Huffs had encouraged students to paint outside regular school hours fourteen years earlier. The commercial aspects of propagating these myths cannot be ignored as the painting production, as well as the crafts production at the SFIS, did much to lure tourists by auto and rail to the shops, galleries, and museums of Santa Fe and the Santa Fe region.

Many publications of the twenties contained information on production of Indian arts and crafts. Various *School Arts* magazines of this period devoted whole issues to Indian arts and crafts being produced throughout the country in BIA and public schools. The February 1932 issue of *Progressive Education* magazine focused on the question of arts education for North American and Mexican Indians, with articles by such noted writers and reformers as John Collier, Julian Huxley, Mary Austin, and Oliver La Farge. These articles as well as those found in other periodicals of the period were well illustrated with photographs of students' work in drawing and painting based on tribal motifs and tribal activities, traditional pottery, weaving, basketry, embroidery, silver and woodcraft, woodblock and linocuts, dioramas or reservation life, and occasional murals.

Such production certainly had been known to Miss Dunn as she too had taught in two BIA day schools before applying to the SFIS for a painting position. The efforts, however, were not as widely publicized and generally known as the efforts of anthropologists Hewett and Chapman and Chapman's protege, Dunn, in bringing Indian students together with Indian artists, anthropologists, and Indian arts collectors to refresh the students' "memories" of their own tribal motifs and designs.

Dunn gives Chester Faris much of the credit for the opening of the painting studio at the school in her account of the "Santa Fe Movement 1932-1937," in her widely circulated book, *American Indian Painting of the Southwest and Plains Area*, published by the University of New Mexico in 1968. One is reminded of Faris' remark in the previous chapter that he first asked the Indians what they wanted, then he attempted to give it to them.

An article on "Vocational Guidance in the Academic Classroom," published in the *Indian School Journal of Chilocco Industrial School* in Oklahoma in January of 1932, makes it quite clear that although the traditional vocations of agriculture, building, printing, baking, and engineering were especially acceptable for boys there, that both boys and girls may now consider a career in the "fine and applied arts" fields at the Chilocco School. This program antedates the studio at Santa Fe by one academic year and had offerings in drawing, design, and cartoon work. "Native Arts" and "Industries" were in the planning stage but a wide variety of music courses were being taught. The article ends with a reminder that,

"All of the courses in the fine and applied arts contribute very materially to the aesthetic and individualistic avocational sides of life and in many instances prove highly remunerative for those who excel in such work."[2]

The remuneration from such works was a well established part of the economy in the Southwest by 1931-32 and had been since the coming of the railways and motor cars. By the time the De Huffs encouraged promising students to paint at the SFIS, the Indian arts and crafts business had been flourishing in and around Santa Fe for twenty-nine years. Edwin Wade, in his study of the Southwest ethnic art market, reports that, "By 1890 the demand for Southwest Indian arts and crafts was outstripping the supply." The commercial success of the San Ildefonso painting and pottery groups, the followers of Crescendio Martinez, the painters who gathered around the SFIS, the School of American Research, The Museum of New Mexico, and the Laboratory of Anthropology at Santa Fe, had convinced entrepreneurs that paintings as well as the "traditional" crafts were as salable as Navajo rugs and Pueblo wedding vases.

The Fred Harvey restaurant and hotel organization was largely responsible for exposing Easterners and Westerners to the Indians of the Southwest and Wade describes this unusual series of events in the following excerpt from his dissertation:

In 1880 the Atchison, Topeka and Santa Fe Railroad came to Albuquerque. During that same year the Atlantic and Pacific Railroad began constructing a line at Isleta that would reach to the West Coast and connect as far east as Oklahoma. Eventually the Pueblo of Laguna would be served by this railway, with a train station right in their village.

The railroad brought large numbers of people into the area. More people than ever before could have personal contact with Pueblo and Navajo Indians. Many had been exposed to museum collections and reports dealing with the indigenous arts of the Southwest, and they came prepared to purchase any ethnic curios they could find. In economic terms, the railroad had produced a regular demand population.

Once aware of this new and burgeoning demand, the Indians responded by expanding production and shaping their products more closely to what tourists wanted. For example, space limitations made it awkward for the train traveler to take home full-size water jars; as a result, Pueblo pottery became smaller. New shapes appeared as well...

Train passengers took their souvenirs back to the East and West Coast, stimulating interest among their friends and families. The railroads furnished Indian artists with mobility in selling their products. Free train passes were given out to artists and craftsmen who would sell their work at the depots in towns like Albuquerque and Gallup. This mobility aided in the promotion and advertising of Indian arts, and at the same time allowed the producers to attain personal exposure to the demands and aesthetic tastes of their buying public. None of the Indian traders could have done as much as the railroad did to publicize Indian art.

The increased tourist trade brought by the railroad held important ramifications for the Indian artist and his work. A new type of buyer was appearing — one who demanded a westernized version of the traditional crafts. Unlike the early museum collectors who wanted the item to be traditional in form, designs and functionality..., the new purchaser was mainly concerned that the item look "Indian."[3]

National reform groups, which had turned their attention in the mid-twenties to the saving of Native American traditions in the arts, were heartened by reports from their representatives in the field.

The Indian reformers had raised the public's consciousness concerning the "plight of the Indian," various artists and writers brought their art to a select public through museum and gallery exhibits, but it seems certain that Henry Ford and Fred Harvey can be greatly credited for disseminating the news of the desirability of collecting Indian arts to the general public and made it possible for them to do so, thereby greatly affecting the quality and quantity of Indian arts production.

Wade states that in 1903 the Fred Harvey organization published "The Indians of the Southwest." The booklet emphasized the variety and quaintness of Indian crafts. Undoubtedly this publicity brochure served to stimulate collecting interest among many of the tourists." A further incentive to collectors was the Fred Harvey Museum which was founded in Albuquerque in 1902. Wade remarks that, "Tourists thrilled to watch real Indians making arts and crafts (there). When these items were offered for sale, they proved irresistible."

Caught up in such a merchandising whirl, the Fred Harvey organization bought nearly half of the Hubbell Arizona Trading Post's Navajo rugs each year, by the pound as was the custom at that time, and sent repeated orders to traders such as J.S. Candelario in Santa Fe to supply the Harvey organization with such items as, "200 assorted small pieces of pottery, which we can sell at retail from $.15 to $.25," and, "one barrel of Rain Gods."

Clearly the time was economically right for the establishment of painting classes at the SFIS when Dorothy Dunn approached

Faris with her proposal to do so in August of 1932.

The time was also politically right as President Hoover had appointed Charles J. Rhoads and J. Henry Scattergood as Commissioner and Assistant Commissioner of Indian Affairs. Bank and college presidents, both Quakers, they were "probably the first ever appointed (to these positions) without regard for party affiliation or political pay-off," states McNickle in *Indian Man*. "These offices were not under Civil Service and had always been regarded as suitable recognition for minor political hackwork."

For almost two years Collier and Rhoads worked together to implement the reforms recommended in the Meriam Report. To assist him in implementing these educational goals, Rhoads appointed Dr. W. Carson Ryan, Jr., a disciple of John Dewey, professor of education at Swarthmore, and former member of the Meriam Commission staff, as director of Indian education.

To implement the recommendations of the Meriam Report, Ryan reduced the non-reservation boarding schools by increasing the number of day schools on reservations and increasing the enrollment of Indian children in public schools near their homes. He increased the number of educational positions in the Indian Service by 800 in 1931. Many of these teachers were more highly qualified than the public school teachers. To assist those teachers who were not, Ryan established summer courses throughout the Indian country and further encouraged staff attendance at local normal colleges.

To attempt to meet these needs in the Southwest, education institutions, such as the University of New Mexico, proposed new courses of study for Pueblo and Navajo students. The September, 1930 issue of *El Palacio* reported that:

> The University of New Mexico, in cooperation with the Laboratory of Anthropology in Santa Fe has been making a study of the present cultural needs of the Indians. It has found that many Indians have marked talent for the arts and crafts, but that the basic knowledge of the true and beautiful in Indian design has been corrupted by the white man's art and that many articles produced are of little decorative value. This fact lowers their sale and demand. If the art of the American Indian is to be encouraged, a number of Indians must be given a thorough training in the principles of Indian design based on the study of the best that has been produced in the past.

> This knowledge is available at this institution through the research of Mr. Kenneth Chapman, of the Laboratory of Anthropology and the University of New Mexico . . . . This training should make

available a number of Indians trained as arts and crafts teachers. The traditional culture of the group to which the individual belongs will be taken into consideration. The student from the Pueblo will be encouraged to follow and develop the designs of his Pueblo, and the Navajo will be directed along the lines of Navajo Art. The students who complete the work will be given certificates of proficiency by the University in lieu of degrees.[4]

The curriculum proposed by Chapman included in addition to the designs of the students' Pueblo or reservation, "sculpture, carving, and wood block printing." Admission was to be open to unmarried students, sixteen to twenty-one years of age, who could "speak fairly good English." The students were to be housed at the Albuquerque Indian School, and their tuition was to be paid by the Indian Bureau at the established rate of sixty cents a day.

Dorothy Dunn was exposed to Kenneth Chapman's work and educational philosophies while she was employed as a day school teacher at Santo Domingo Pueblo, south of Santa Fe, New Mexico. Dunn remarks, "While still a student of the Art Institute of Chicago (1925), a growing interest in Indian art led me to seek the rather adventurous position of grade school teacher for the U.S. Indian Service at two New Mexican posts — first at Santo Domingo Pueblo, and two years later at the Navajo Agency at Shiprock." She further comments that, "In these full years I gained an introduction to Southwest Indian culture, and began the teaching of art which was to be my life's work. At the same time, I was able to pursue formal studies of American Indian art at the University of New Mexico."

Dunn lived and worked at Santo Domingo for two years. While there she became intensely interested in teaching language and social studies through the arts and in encouraging her students to use their sense of color and design in various classroom projects. Looking back on her experience in 1931, Dunn comments that, "There was a course of study, standard in Indian schools, regular public texts and certain 'rules and regulations' which I regretted but determined to make the best of by adapting them when practicable and forgetting their existence when not."[5]

Dunn's story from the Santo Domingo period on has been told and retold by herself and others as they attributed the beginning of the painting studio at the SFIS and the arts philosophy surrounding it to Dunn's efforts and the foresight and tolerance of Supt. Chester Faris. In a recent retelling, Dunn recalls:

Following a year's final study at the Art Institute, where I earned my diploma and integrated what I had learned during my self-determined internship at the government schools, I planned a return to the Southwest. When in August 1932 there were still no painting classes at the Santa Fe Indian school, I outlined my project ideas to the Superintendent, Chester Faris. He was receptive but puzzled as to how to launch such a program as there was no "art teaching position under Civil Service." Mr. Faris suggested I apply to Washington for a fifth-grade vacancy, "if you think you could handle both grade teaching *and* the painting classes." Meanwhile the school had a small fund available for odd labor; could I start my project as a "laborer" at forty dollars a month? I was indeed willing to begin on any terms, with the firm conviction that the Studio I had in mind could help the younger, oncoming talent to express itself.[6]

The new painting studio opened, although unofficially, in the Santa Fe Indian School on September 9, 1932. Within a year the Studio program had attracted so many students and so much community and national interest, that Dunn was given an official Bureau of Indian Affairs title as "Teacher of Fine and Applied Arts," the first such designation in the Bureau.

The new Arts and Crafts Building at the SFIS was opened in the spring of 1931; Faris, in the spring of 1932, engaged muralist Olive Rush and her assistant Louise Morris to supervise a group of established Santa Fe Indian artists, aided by students at the SFIS, to paint large figurative murals in the manner of the modern Pueblo painters on the walls of the cafeteria. Dunn's book, *American Indian Painting of the Southwest and Plains Areas,* contains a lengthy and complete description of the mural painting activity from information shared with Dunn by the mural painters and her friend Olive Rush. (See Dunn pages 243-249.) Sections of the mural were exhibited in New York, Gallup, New Mexico, and the Century of Progress Exhibit in Chicago. Although succeeding generations at the school have altered the murals somewhat, they remain essentially intact and may be viewed with permission by the inquiring scholar as may the other extant murals done under Dorothy Dunn's direction.

It is important to note that under Faris' direction, the Bureau sanctioned an Arts and Crafts Department and the murals brought regional and national attention to the school through sales, exhibits, and articles written in literary and scholarly journals about the school's activities, by such writers as Mary Austin, Olive Rush, and Erna Fergusson, before the painting studio was well established. The vitality of the early twenties, which had been focused by artists and writers of the Santa Fe area on the Bursum Bill, and on the threatened banishment by the federal bureaucracy of religious practice and dances on the reservations, could now be focused on the SFIS and its role in promulgating and promoting the "traditional" arts, which was of utmost importance to these individuals and groups, and the underlying reason that many had fought so valiantly for reform in Indian matters. To save the "traditional arts" was to save the "traditional culture"; to save the "traditional culture" was to "save the Indian."

The Arts and Crafts Department, the painting studio, and other improvements and additions at the SFIS were typical of the changes in Bureau education under Ryan's direction. Appropriations were set by Congress allowing more funding for food and clothing in the boarding schools. Student discipline procedures were closely scrutinized and guarded, the uniform course of study was modified to more adequately meet the needs of the community served, and civil service positions in the Bureau were upgraded. For the first time a division in the Bureau was created that dealt with Indian education only. Closer ties were encouraged with each state in supervising the BIA educational activities within its boundaries, regional control of BIA institutions was emphasized over direct control from Washington, more community schools were developed, and some unsuitable boarding schools were closed. The Rhoads period during President Hoover's administration effected some of the most significant changes in Indian education to date.

Ryan's emphasis on industrial training geared to meet the job market, reinforced Faris' and other boarding school supervisors' decisions to emphasize the "fine" and "practical arts" and the "Native Industries" wherever such course offerings would provide appropriate career skills. Santa Fe proved to be such a place and although the past administrators had been slow or reluctant to initiate these skills, or actually forbidden at times to do so, the SFIS of the early 1930's soon became the model for other Bureau schools throughout Indian country which hoped to use its methods in their state or region to provide job opportunities for their graduates in arts and related activities.

In direct contrast to the activities of the Studio, life went on at the school until the late fifties much as it had from the beginning. Brody comments that, "Conditions were certainly less repressive in the 1930's than earlier, but they were still far from ideal, and the patterns for acceptable behavior had become well established. They [the boarding schools] were hardly places in which creativity could have been expected."[7] Because of the continued scheduled half days in the classroom, half days in manual labor, some students painted an hour a day, and only after all other duties were accomplished. Uniforms, marching, bells to rise by, eat by, work by, to study and retire by persisted past the middle thirties. But for those fortunate to have the attention of Dunn and her friends and supporters, the early thirties were a time of experiment and discovery and oftentimes rebellion.

Dunn's influence over the students at the SFIS during the years 1932-1937 was and is in many ways incalculable as that influence still manifests itself in the art programs of Indian day schools, public high schools, boarding school art departments, and on the walls of museums and galleries throughout the world. She had the good fortune to be accepted into the proper institutional environment at the most opportune time to accomplish the goals she had set for herself.

Dunn would never be able to resolve for herself or her students the philosophic contradictions of the goals and objectives she had set for the Studio: researching one's own tribal background for inspiration and motif, attempting to develop in one's own culture as an idiosyncratic artist, without outside tribal or "academic influence", and the possibility or indeed the inevitability that a developing artist would wish to go beyond tribal and ethnic bonds. She, in fact, did all she could in her well-intentioned instruction to avoid such a possibility, hoping to keep the whole of art produced by Indians intact, tribally untainted, and as historically understandable as the pots lined up neatly on the shelves at the Laboratory of Anthropology. Dunn states that to accomplish her goals and objectives she developed a "broad plan of procedure (that) was 1) to determine insofar as possible, each student's personality, interests, abilities, the backgrounds of his tribal art and its relationship to his individual art and the general arts, 2) without teaching in the formal sense, to create a guidance technique which would provide motivation, clarification and development for each individual student's painting process."

She felt in most instances that her students had not been exposed to the best of their own tribal art or the best of art of other countries, and she was committed, as Hewett and Chapman, to "establishing (Indian Art) in its rightful place as one of the fine arts of the world." She soon found that her most difficult task was to convince her students that their own tribal arts were legitimate art and that it was permissible to produce paintings, keeping in mind one's own tribal design taboos, outside the reservation.

Friction developed between the director of the arts and crafts department and Dunn over the philosophy of the painting studio. The crafts director who was employed at the SFIS when the cafeteria murals were done, felt that the Studio's paintings should be large, drawn from live models, and more teacher directed. Dunn disagreed, adhered steadfastly to her goals and admitted quite frankly that the paintings were small because materials were in such short supply. To appease the director, Dunn set up nighttime classes with a live model but these extra-academic classes were not on the whole well-attended and she dropped them after a few weeks, convinced that the Indian students preferred to paint from memory, as firmly convinced of this perception as she was that her students should not use value, light, and shade in their work. Dunn felt that Indian school art departments had an obligation to keep Indian art untouched by other influences.

In her first year Dunn administered to her forty students a rudimentary subject matter test to assess their interests and concluded that to meet the needs of such a varied ethnic, age, and formal background group that she must begin with basic instruction in color, design, handling of brushes and watercolor paints. Many of the exercises she gave the students could easily have come from any art fundamentals class.

After accomplishing these exercises the students were encouraged to reproduce scenes from their Pueblos and reservations. For inspiration they drew on design and color "memories" of pots, baskets, costumes, and other arts works essential to their own tribal culture. For those who could not remember, there were books, drawings, and photographs readily available for their research and study. Dunn supplemented these materials with historical works she felt complemented the "Indian style." Especially interesting to her students, Dunn states, were Paleolithic painting, Egyptian frescoes, East Indian miniatures, and Chinese watercolors.

In an officially sanctioned institutional setting, Dunn was fulfilling the role that anthropologists, traders, and other educators had partially and widely filled in the past. Not only was she providing materials and encouragement to the young artists, but arts guidance and research as well. These student artists were housed, fed, clothed, and provided with the time and place to practice their arts with the approval of the federal government, the interest of Indian arts support groups, and an enthusiastic buying public. No longer must they scratch out their efforts on or with any materials available, no longer must they work surreptitiously after school hours, or at menial jobs to support their painting. Indian painting had become a fully institutionalized activity, one that quickly would bring more public and financial recognition to the SFIS students than any activities engaged in by Bureau students in the past, and an activity that would also greatly speed their acculturation into the white mainstream of society.

The SFIS had become, for the Bureau and public, the official arts and crafts school for all Indian groups and students soon came in large numbers to avail themselves of the opportunity to train there.

The paintings that were produced continued to be in the tradition of earlier modern painters, many of whom had attended the SFIS and still lived in the Santa Fe area. The San Ildefonso group and its followers, the painters of the Kiowa school which developed under the guidance of Bureau matron Susan Peters in Oklahoma, almost concurrently with the Pueblo group, served as models for the young students, along with their research into their own tribal arts.

As the Studio began to receive requests for shows here and abroad, the students under Dunn's direction learned marketing and social skills, as they worked out publicity materials and attended their own openings or went on tour with a show. The commercial aspects of such shows were heartily encouraged by the Bureau and the Indian Arts and Crafts Board.

The Indian Arts and Crafts Board was established by Congress in 1935 to promote through native Indian products the economic welfare of American Indians. The Board was given powers, among them the right to engage in various types of technical and merchandising research, to study market conditions, and where practicable, to adopt and establish trade marks for Indian products guaranteeing genuineness and quality.

The public warmly and enthusiastically embraced the Studio style which consisted of depictions of tribal activities executed in positive color images on a white or neutral, negative ground. The figures were laid in with flat clear opaque color and in most cases outlined crisply in black. Many unified motifs were chosen: figures, animals, birds. Others were unrelated actual Indian tribal based designs. The student had been discouraged from crossing tribal barriers for designs and criticized for being "unauthentic." But tribal lines were crossed and symbols readily invented. Chemical as well as natural earth-derived colors were used and the painter felt no obligation to be naturalistic. Some teacher-artists, such as Allan Houser balked at Dunn's painting philosophy but most capitulated, as the Studio style was the prevailing and most commercially

51

successful mode of Indian painting.[8]

In 1934 Chester Faris, accompanied by twenty-six students from the SFIS representing twelve tribes, toured the Southeast and Washington, D.C. by bus and car, taking with them a large collection of student watercolors which were shown at the Southeast Fair at Atlanta. In Washington the students were received by dignitaries and were said to have made "quite a stir as they walk(ed) down Pennsylvania Avenue wearing their gorgeous costumes."

Some of the students represented in this group were Marie [sic] Martinez, San Ildefonso; Velino Herrera, Zia; Teisefor Reyna, Taos; Geronima Cruz, San Juan; John Lucero, Isleta; Manuelito, Navajo; and Martin Vigil, Tesuque. Marie Martinez, potter, already the holder of two medals from the Century of Progress, captivated the large crowd in attendance with her quiet manner and graceful pottery demonstration. The *New Mexican* quotes the *Atlanta Constitution* as saying that Marie "is one of the talented Indians contributing to the enlightenment of the thousands of pale faces who are visiting the (fair) Indian village daily."

Back at the school, the painting classes quickly grew in size and recognition. Notables such as Frederick H. Douglas, Curator of Indian Art at the Denver Museum, came and gave it his "professional approval," Dunn says. New and larger quarters were provided for the Studio, a regular budget designated for supplies and equipment, and one-half of the monies collected from the sale of student works was put into a fund to supply the Studio's gallery needs. The Museum of New Mexico established a yearly show of the students' work which was for many years given a lengthy review in *El Palacio* by supportive writers in Santa Fe. The paper, *Indians at Work*, published by the BIA under John Collier, carried frequent articles on the school, as did numerous educational publications. Dunn wrote tirelessly of the school's program, causing artists, educators, and museum directors to visit its program. Numerous shows were sent out yearly by Dunn and her students to Washington, D.C., the major museums and galleries of the United States, and to many countries abroad. The Santa Fe Indian Arts Fund and the New Mexico Association on Indian Affairs continued to support the school's efforts through shows, lectures, publications, and monetary gifts and purchases. As news of the student mural activity at the school spread, the Studio began to receive requests for murals from New Mexico to Washington, D.C., and many of the students, such as Pablita Velarde from Santa Clara Pueblo, gained reputations as fine muralists before leaving school.

A number of significant happenings in 1934 affected the population of the SFIS: The Johnson-O'Malley Act was put in force by Congress, the formation of the Indian Arts and Crafts Board was recommended, and the Indian Re-organization Act was finally passed. In this same year, the courageous and farsighted Chester Faris was transferred to Window Rock, Arizona to become the General Superintendent of the Navajo Tribe. In his last term at the SFIS he officiated at its first high school graduation.

The Indian Re-organization Act helped to calm and settle many of the old land disputes in the Southwest and heralded a new era of self-determination for its Indian peoples. The Johnson-O'Malley Act laid the groundwork for Indian involvement and self-determination in matters of education and various other areas of reservation concern. The formation of the Indian Arts and Crafts Board in 1935 helped to establish the Indian as an authentic craftsperson, with rules and regulations defining and controlling the quality, price and identification of Indian produced products. The Pueblo peoples, braced by this series of events, formed formal organizations to promote their own welfare.

The loss of Faris to the Navajo Nation would shortly be felt at the SFIS. After a year with an interim superintendent, J.B. Vernon, the school was consolidated with other Pueblo agencies to form the United Pueblos Agency, signalling the problems in shared governance which continued to plague the SFIS and its successor, The Institute of American Indian Arts, for more than forty-five years.

In 1935 Dr. Sophie D. Aberle was appointed General Superintendent of the North and South United Pueblo Agency. Dr. Aberle was on loan from Johns Hopkins University and the Carnegie Institute in Washington, D.C. to study Indian affairs in the Southwest. In 1936, Dr. C.H. Seymour was appointed as the Superintendent of the Santa Fe and Albuquerque Indian Schools, and a new era in the schools' management began.

Meanwhile, the Studio continued to thrive. By 1938 almost every Indian painter of any note had attended the Studio: Oscar Howe, Allan Houser, Jose Toledo, Pablita Velarde, Fred Kabotie, Harrison Begay, Pop-Chalee, Quincy Tahoma, Maria Martinez, Kiowa artist, Jack Hokeah, and many others. Studios were set up in other Bureau schools using the Santa Fe model, and the Studio's influence was felt everywhere Indians were taught. When tracing the backgrounds of older notable Indian artists of today, one will find they attended the studio, or a school patterned after it, were taught by a Studio artist, or in some way were directly influenced by an artist or the art emanating from the Studio.

In 1935 Paul Coze, French painter, writer, and ethnologist, arranged a show of one hundred watercolors from the school to be shown at the Trocadero Institute of Ethnology in Paris. A thousand viewers in evening attire turned out for the opening. Coze states, "The American Ambassador was there — also other notables of the diplomatic corps; also warriors, musicians, letterateurs and financiers." Coze explained the European, especially the German, fascination with the Indian as stemming from the novels of James Fenimore Cooper, the Buffalo Bill shows, and all articles, books and posters of Indians available in Europe. Coze wrote upon his return to Santa Fe that he saw the Indian in America "as a true artist first," and he felt that the Indian "would move into many media, that he would bring to America an art of his own soon, and that this art would be a collaboration and amalgam of the art of the white and red man which would produce the real American art."

Shows such as this built the demand for shows from the SFIS to such a magnitude that Dunn says that she and her students and student teachers had difficulty providing them. As many as thirty shows were requested in a year's time.

When Seymour took up his official position as superintendent in 1936, the *New Mexican* reported on Seymour's intentions for the schools in Santa Fe and Albuquerque under his charge:

> Arts and crafts will be emphasized at the Santa Fe Indian School, agriculture at Albuquerque. Subjects that are not related to the pupils lives, such as higher math and foreign languages, are being eliminated and emphasis is being placed on better English, both as to vocabulary and fluency which he explained is essential to their lives.
>
> Every child in the Santa Fe school is being given some craftwork. The silversmith class is greatly increased this year and Miss Dunn's painting class has nearly 300 pupils. The woodworking has been put on a better footing with simple, appropriate designs, and hardwood with which to work for the first time. This wood is particularly designed for furniture which sees much work. [9]

Seymour also explained a new system whereby a student might work for room and board one day a week and attend school the other four. He assured his teachers that they would be retained from year to year if they merited retention, alluding to a charge from the teachers that they had not been assured of this sort of job security in the past. A news release from the SFIS a few days earlier noted that four hundred students were in attendance there, that the school now consisted of the seventh to twelfth grades only, that industrial training was being reorganized, and that "Indian painting and design and not handicrafts (would) receive emphasis in the program." "Students," the article stated, "would be accepted from New Mexico, California, and Arizona only, with some exceptions." Under Seymour and the United Pueblo Agencies, the school began to draw in on itself and became regionalistic. In time, this regionalism would contribute to its decline and demise.

As interest in woven art products, basketry, and jewelry waned, painting was gaining a larger and larger market. Santa Fe, now a growing capital city of almost fourteen thousand, continued to be the center and prototype for Indian sales and exhibit activity surrounding Indian school painting.

Although the opportunity for three-fourths of the SFIS students to paint or engage in crafts was available, this was still a boarding school, still a place far from home and family and all that was familiar; and although most students came willingly, many of the inadequacies of boarding school life that persisted before the thirties lingered on after it became an arts and crafts school. Pablita Velarde explains that her comings and goings at the school were caused partially because the school provided clothing and that made it easier for her father to provide for his children. [10]

Carmelita Dunlap, San Ildefonso potter, tells a touching and amusing story of how she attended the SFIS a full year before her family knew where she was. In the fall a bus would pick up children from the northern pueblos to be delivered to St. Catherine's Boarding School in Santa Fe and the SFIS. Her family had planned that she would spend the year at St. Catherine's, but she, wanting to paint and be with other members of her family, got off the bus at the SFIS stop. Although her home at San Ildefonso was only twenty-five miles away, it was a lengthy journey at that time, and as no one came to visit her throughout the year, her secret was kept until the following summer. [11]

Although it is seldom mentioned, when School enrollments dropped in the late thirties and early forties, non-Indian children were allowed to attend the SFIS by special arrangement with the school superintendent. Mrs. Allan Houser, former IAIA staff member, explained that parents encouraged this arrangement because some of the schools of northern New Mexico were so academically poor at the time, and they wanted their children to learn to speak and write English properly. One suspects that many parents in these hard times, given the opportunity for free room and board, medical services, clothing, transportation, and school supplies for their children, risked the problems of placing them in a segregated school society so that they might have proper care as well as schooling.

By the fall of 1937, stories relating to the SFIS had virtually disappeared from the pages of the *Santa Fe New Mexican*. The Indian Arts Fund and the New Mexico Association on Indian Affairs met from time to time, but the SFIS had slipped from prominence in the news. Instead, speculation concerning the activities of Hitler and Mussolini and the Japanese seemed to spread to every inch of type, and arts activities became more and more relegated to gossip and society columns.

The November 9, 1937 *New Mexican* carried a small article, the title of which nearly equalled the narrative in length: "Geronima Cruz, Only Indian Member of State Art Teachers' Association Interprets Her People in Address." Geronima had made a presentation to the art teachers of New Mexico in Santa Fe. Her presentation consisted of a discussion of the arts of a number of tribes, and of showing examples of their work. The reporter, obviously impressed with her presentation, states with admiration that, "Miss Cruz, a recent graduate of the Santa Fe Indian School and formerly associate art teacher, is the youngest member of the State Art Teachers' Association and its only Indian member."

The Dorothy Dunn era at the SFIS was drawing to a close. She says of 1937, her fifth year, "The objectives of the Studio had largely been achieved. It was an instrument for the guidance and development of artists, and an agency for enlisting the interest of the public in Indian painting . . . Climaxing the final year under my guidance, the Studio was awarded a bronze medal at the 1937 International Exposition of Arts and Techniques in Paris." Olive Rush, who wrote the review for the annual SFIS student show at the Museum of New Mexico, perceives Cruz' coming role when she says, "Assisting . . . the work to keep it purely Indian and uncommercial is Geronima Cruz of San Juan, a former student who has charge of the young pupils. At the studio there is an entire roomful of the work of her pupils, excellent in standard for children so young." Dunn says simply, "Thereafter, the students took over the work of the Studio entirely, with Po-Tsunu (Geronima Cruz Montoya) of the San Juan Pueblo, herself an Indian artist and former student, placed in charge. She was ably assisted in the beginning by Ha-So-De (Narciso Abeita), Jose Ray Toledo, and others. In the years to come, Indian artists increasingly led and directed the evolution of Indian art themselves, and many outstanding students appeared at the Indian School in Santa Fe to refine and develop their talents. Po-Tsunu directed the Studio for nearly twenty-five years."

The years following Dunn's retirement until the closing down of the SFIS program in 1962 were quiet and uneventful in comparison with the events surrounding the early years at the school. Dunn continued to write and lecture about her experiences in Santa Fe and about the artists who had come out of the Studio period. Her writings helped to keep the Studio concept alive in art and educational publications throughout the late forties and middle fifties. The Museum of New Mexico continued yearly shows of work of the student artists and occasional shows were sent out from the school.

By the advent of World War II, the SFIS, except for the coverage of its sports activities, had slipped into almost total anonymity. A complex system of supervision had developed at the school with the appointment of Seymour in 1936, consisting of an area director or superintendent of education, usually Albuquerque-based, assisted in Santa Fe and at the Albuquerque Indian School by either a school superintendent or principal. It appears that along with Pueblo Indian introversion, the complicated chain of command made action at the local level more difficult to initiate and somewhat encumbered community involvement and publicity. The Arts and Crafts Department established a salesroom at the school, supervised by the department head, assisted by the students. The Arts and Crafts Department continued its program until 1958.

The painting classes, now simply referred to as "art" classes, continued on as a part of the vocational program until 1959 when the classes were separated from the academic vocational program. Geronima Cruz Montoya worked with the painting classes for most of the period from Dunn's retirement in 1937 until the advent of the Institute of American Indian Arts program in 1962. She and her assistants attempted to follow Dunn's objectives throughout their stay.

The Indian Arts and Crafts Board continued to be aggressive in its goals throughout this period although from time to time it lacked an acting director. During the war years when toursim was down and materials such as wool and silver were controlled by the federal government, the Board sought and received, on behalf of the Indian craftsperson, exceptions to these restrictions, and wisely set up regional, multi-tribal arts and crafts shows to open new markets. To further sanction and institutionalize the production of arts and crafts in the schools and on the reservations, the Interior Department established a gallery in its building in Washington D.C. in which to show frequently changing exhibits of Indian life and arts.

The Pueblo Indians were very much concerned with the activities of the Indian Arts and Crafts Board, as evidence by a story in the *New Mexican* during John Collier's term as Indian Commissioner in 1941. Collier, in Santa Fe to make a presentation to the All-Pueblo Council, was severely criticized by those present concerning the lack of Indian representation on the Indian Arts and Crafts Board. The Pueblo Indians felt they had made a strong public statement of support for their arts and crafts when in 1939 they had built, at the State Fairgrounds in Albuquerque, a building in which to show Pueblo work, saying that they had chosen to do so, "to foster the arts and crafts of the Pueblo peoples and further their education."

During the Santa Fe Fiesta in 1941, for the first time, a number of Pueblo artists held their own independent show in Santa Fe at the Hall of Ethnology on Washington Street. The Hall of Ethnology had been recently opened under the direction of Bertha Dutton, ethnologist and writer. This independent effort was the third such show for Harrison Begay during the Fiesta, but that he was joined by others was a significant event. Those showing painting and silverwork with Begay were Ignacio Moquino, Percy Tsesete, J.C. Herrera, Quincy Tahoma, Justin Herrera, and Joe Quintana. These independent efforts on the part of the Pueblo artists, plus the Department of Interior shows and those supplied by Santa Fe gallery owners to galleries outside of the Southwest region, continued to give the Studio artist a new and enthusiastic audience and built collections of their and their followers' works for those who had expressed an interest in the Studio and its efforts over the years.

It is most unfortunate that although Pueblo and other Indian students had the opportunity for arts training in their years at the SFIS, few went on to higher education in the arts. In the mid-thirties, of the 204 Indian students enrolled in colleges and universities, only 8 were enrolled in art programs. Even though the Indian students at the SFIS had been exposed to progressive concepts in education through Bureau education directors, Ryan and Beatty, those students who went on for further training in the arts during this period were rare. Those who did go on for further training usually returned to their home areas or to the SFIS to teach. Few truly outgrew or surpassed the tenets of their earlier Studio training, and many would gradually drift into other fields. Indeed, most SFIS graduates of the late thirties and early forties returned to their reservations to settle into a semi-rural, semi-urban existence around the small towns of the Southwest. Of these, many supplemented their incomes with work at their painting and crafts, and the most practiced and dedicated provided for themselves and their families in this manner. Commissioner Collier explained to the Pueblo Indians in 1941 that the Bureau's "education efforts now were aimed at fitting Indians to live on their lands and not for professional careers."

Collier, however, couldn't have anticipated the effects of World War II on the Indian population: the loss of young men and women to the war, the new mobility brought on by recruitment of service people and defense workers, the demand for new kinds of industrial training to be used in war-spawned industries, and the necessity for a multitude of academic training areas to be financed for the returning service men and women by the G.I. Bill.

The SFIS was never successful in meeting the challenges of the post-war period. It had not thrown itself into defense training or the supplying of foodstuffs to the Bureau during the war as other boarding schools had, but had continued with the curriculum established for it in the early thirties.

While most federal boarding schools' populations had dropped dramatically during the war, Santa Fe's had remained consistent. As with other schools, it found some of its students and staff going to the service, and budget and personnel cuts necessitated by a wartime budget difficult to deal with, but its status as an arts and crafts school, with an established and well-publicized painting department, kept it somewhat isolated from the wartime difficulties of other boarding schools. After the war, when other boarding schools found their populations suddenly rising, Santa Fe's diminished and the nature of its student body changed. Its curriculum wasn't the sort that students of the fifties and their families sought out: the traditional crafts, agriculture, woodworking, and so on were being replaced in other schools by high school technical training and emphasis on the science and college preparatory courses. More and more, Pueblo students were seeking out such training in their area public junior and senior high schools. By the middle fifties, the SFIS was little more than a dumping ground for "trouble" and "problem" students from many reservations; in the vernacular of the times, "juvenile delinquents."

While other boarding schools were upgrading their curriculum, Santa Fe's had changed only in small ways. During the last decade other tribal groups, especially the Navajo, had begun to produce educational materials in their own language, providing the groundwork for cross-cultural studies. The SFIS, Pueblo dominated and supervised, had not yet begun to investigate these possibilities for its various tribal groups. In point of fact, the SFIS students' seemed to prefer the type of training that their parents had experienced at SFIS, and the parents preferred it for their children. The fact that the Southwest Indian artist or craftsperson, unlike Indians in other parts of the country, had not lost their market during the war, although sales dropped as tourism dropped, helped to reinforce the old curriculum at the SFIS and impeded change. Santa Fe had remained, through all political and economic changes, the undisputed center for sales of Indian arts and crafts. Its galleries, museums, Indian Markets, Fiestas, and public enterprises had kept the market up and demand continuing for "things Indian."

In an attempt to save the SFIS, an amazing number of class additions and subtractions had taken place in the fifties. Ordinarily serving grades seven through twelve, the school administration changed the emphasis to grades five through twelve in 1958, six through nine from 1959 through the spring of 1962. In the fall of 1958 the entire high school was transferred to Albuquerque and the fifth and sixth grades were transferred from San Felipe Pueblo to the SFIS to join the remaining seventh and eighth grades. In 1959 the arts and crafts department was removed entirely, leaving only the painting classes in the academic/vocational program. In the fall of 1960, a newly organized arts and crafts department, totally separate from the academic/vocational program, was opened to high school graduates, or those over eighteen, from all over the United States. The ninth grade class of 1961-62 was the highest grade level to matriculate at the SFIS.

All these changes seemed to serve no real purpose. The school's academic and art program had slipped so badly that opening it up to a broader group of students was not the answer. All these seesawing changes were difficult for the staff and faculty to adjust to. Indians, who had been given preference in hiring in the Reorganization Act of 1934, found themselves being subtly eased out of their civil service positions in the late forties, to make room for white personnel. The academic/vocational training that remained had to be focused on a younger troup of students each year; the upper grades had been moved to Albuquerque where there had been an emphasis on vocational training for twenty years, and no special areas of training had been established for adults other than arts and crafts.

A new directon was desperately needed if the physical campus was to continue to serve in its capacity as an "industrial school", as it was designated by the City of Santa Fe in its original charter. That change would take place in the fall of 1962 with the official opening of the Institute of American Indian Arts program replacing the old SFIS program.

The Pueblo Indians had lost their control of the campus after a twenty-seven year administration. This campus, on Cerrillos Road in Santa Fe, originally donated to Rev. Horatio Ladd and his first University of New Mexico, which he and his Christian supporters had turned over to the Bureau of Indian Affairs as the site for the Santa Fe Indian Industrial School, would house for the next nineteen years the nation's only all-Indian, all-arts training center. This institute would be the first to be controlled aned supervised by the Indian Arts and Crafts Board, funded directly by the Washington Bureau of Indian Affairs, and opened to all Indians of North America, Eskimos, and Aleuts of one-fourth Indian blood heritage.

III
THE INSTITUTE OF AMERICAN INDIAN ARTS 1962-1970

When I was in charge as Superintendent of the Institute, I felt that our raw materials were not paint, canvas and other art supplies. I felt our responsibility was to lead youth, and that, persons were our product. Art was a by-product. (Geroge Boyce, Santa Fe *New Mexican*, July 21, 1968.)

The mythology that built up around the beginnings of the Studio under Dorothy Dunn's direction at the old Santa Fe Indian School pales in comparison with the ever-increasing mythology which was built up around the creation of the Institute of American Indian Arts (IAIA) on the Santa Fe Indian School campus. Persons and institutions who had played no part in its formation have repeatedly been credited for some aspects or all aspects of its beginning. In July of 1972 Dr. George Boyce, Superintendent of the Institute of American Indian Arts from 1962 until 1966, annoyed by repeated misinformation in the media, wrote the following detailed letter to a reporter at the Santa Fe *New Mexican*, hoping to lay to rest the suppositions surrounding the Institute's beginnings. Before presenting the letter to the reporter, he sought approval by sending it to his long-time friend, Hildegard Thompson, past BIA Director of Indian education. Mrs. Thompson replied immediately that it was a "good letter."[1] As this letter is of utmost historical significance to the study of the Institute of American Indian Arts and was intended by its author to be published as a public document, it is printed in its entirety.

July 23, 1972

Miss Lynne Waugh
c/o The New Mexican
202 N. Marcy
Santa Fe, NM 87501

Dear Miss Waugh:

I have enjoyed your articles on the Institute of American Indian Arts, however, today I am writing to call to your attention some misleading and false statements in the opening of your article entitled 'IAIA

Nurtures Indian Art,' which appeared in the Sunday, July 23, issue on p. 3 of The Arts section.

You state: 'The Institute of American Indian Art (IAIA) grew out of a Rockefeller funded school, which Lloyd New, the noted Indian craftsman, established in Scottsdale, Ariz., in the 1950's. The Department of the Interior's Indian Arts and Crafts Board took it over in 1960 and moved it to Santa Fe two years later. Lloyd New came with it and has been its director ever since.'

The truth has never been told. Your statements are far from the truth. How and where you obtained them I do not know, the true story follows in detail.

1. Initially complaints had been registered in the 1950's by Indian traders and by persons concerned with good Indian art by Indian artists to the Bureau of Indian Affairs (BIA) for its decreased interest and lack of support in this field when Glenn Emmons was Commissioner of Indian Affairs. At that time, Mr. Emmons was imposing more and more emphasis upon the three R's as educational policy for Indians. Rene D'Harnencourt, then Director of the Museum of Modern Art in New York City, and first chairman of the Indian Arts and Crafts Board, which was established as a separate agency under Secretary of the Interior Harold Ickes, requested a meeting with Mr. Emmons to discuss this matter. I was present at that meeting, along with some others as a small group. So was a top official from the office of the Interior Secretary.

2. Obviously under embarrassment and pressure as he departed from the meeting, Mr. Emmons turned to Mrs. Hildegard Thompson, Director of Indian Education, as she followed him down the hall. Mr. Emmons verbally authorized Mrs. Thompson to start a school of some sort for Indian artists. He gave no prescription and departed from the meeting. In this rather offhanded manner what is now IAIA was born.

3. As a consequence, a small art department was set up at the old Santa Fe Indian School which ran for two years but was underfinanced and limited to about 20 young-adult students. I recommended that Miss Mary Mitchell be appointed to head it up when asked by the Washington office for such a person. The Rockefeller Foundation and Lloyd New's activites at that time were never mentioned or considered, although I have personally known Lloyd and his activities in Phoenix and Scottsdale for some 30 years.

4. Being unsatisfied with the operation, Mrs. Hildegard Thompson, in

63

1960, persistently placed and replaced after removal from the BIA's budget request several times, a sum of under a million dollars for capital expenditures for new construction and remodeling at the old Santa Fe School into functioning as an art school, together with pertinent equipment. The School, as yet unplanned in any detail, was essentially justified as an effort to meet unmet needs of a certain group of Indian youths. Mrs. Thompson took the position that if the BIA were to run an art school for Indians, it should be done on a much broader and better basis than was the case with the limping art department that had been authorized by Mr. Emmons, but for which he sought no funds. Had it not been for Mrs. Thompson's persistancy, there would not have been an IAIA.

5. The capital sum was requested by Mrs. Thompson and was approved by Congress. I was again invited to Washington to help pre-plan basic policies in the broadest sense, without specific details at the time. These basic recommendations were then approved in Washington, including a name for the school.

6. Actions by Congress in approving such a school and authorizing the appropriation to get it started were late. I was asked in the summer of 1961 to come to Santa Fe for several weeks from Brigham City, Utah, where I was Superintendent of Intermountain Indian Schools' special program for unschooled Navajo teenagers. I prepared a study of needs based upon a general reconnaissance, and at that time was asked to serve as initial Superintendent of what was soon to become IAIA-as Congress acted.

I transferred here in the early fall of 1961 to do a year of pre-planning. I was given the opportunity to work up all details, within the budget, in planning new construction and remodeling for the new program functions, to also set up an organization for operation of the school, to recruit the staff accordingly and to work up and direct the many unsettled details as to 'what is an art school for Indians' and to equip it accordingly. There were no textbooks of direct prior experience to follow. Girls and boys? How many? What approaches in philosophy? What tribes? And so on, all had to be answered. There were no previous commitments by the BIA.

7. During 1961, I made estimates of operating costs for a student body of around 300. An appropriation for opening the fall of 1962, under a modest budget, was passed by Congress.

8. The entire issue of there being an art school of any sort for Indians,

particularly in Santa Fe, had meanwhile become locally and unexpectedly very controversial. There was a serious question as to whether the proposed school would ever be launched. The first year (1962-63), the plant was severely overcrowded, under a political 'compromise' by Indian Commissioner Phileo Nash. For that year, nearly 200 Navajo and Apache elementary pupils, with a handful of Pueblo pupils — all welfare and social problem children who could best be served nearer their homes — were kept at Santa Fe with the first art students of high school and post-high ages.

9. In recruiting for a head of the art department, I looked over a number of potential persons, including a special visit to Scottsdale to confer with Lloyd New as a possibility. He finally accepted. His title, like the other department heads, was Director. Thus there was an Academic Director, a Home-Living and Guidance Director, a Plant Mangement Director, a Business Administration Director and a Director of the Arts Department, which was Mr. New. Only in this sense was he a 'first' Director, as were the others in their respective departments. He was a Director only of the one Department.

The Indian Arts and Crafts Board was enthusiastic over the concepts being developed. We worked closely with the Board and held meetings with both individual members and the committee as a whole. Following my retirement in the summer of 1966, Frederick J. Dockstader, acting as Chairman of Board, presented me with a citation of confirmation, reading in part:

'. . . .When the Bureau of Indian Affairs established the Institute of American Indian Arts at Santa Fe, you were called upon to initiate and administer the organization of this new concept for American Indian education. The success of your work in the founding of this unique institution has been a major influence in the development of contemporary Indian artists and craftsmen, evidenced by the many young Indian men and women graduating each year who are achieving world-wide renown in their creative work.'

In passing, my own strong feeling was that youths in any vocation today, particularly artists and particularly young Indians need to be stimulated to pursuing further education, academically and for social acceptance. If your product was to be well-rounded persons, then equal emphasis needed to be placed upon creative approaches to academic and behavioral education, with new approaches to art instruction as a route at IAIA.

This seemed to me to be particularly important at the high school level, if more Indian youths were to be redirected to more on-going goals which many lacked in coming to IAIA — and before it was too late. With few exceptions, staffs of all departments accepted and worked in implementation of this principle. The school did prove remarkably successful, as Mr. New has frequently indicated, students immediately won national and international recognition in all fields and media being offered in the arts.

10. In the summer of 1966, I voluntarily retired. Mr. Howard Mackey, then Director of the Academic Department, was appointed as acting Superintendent, as my successor for one year.

11. In the fall of 1967, Mr. Mackey was transferred to Roswell, N.M., for other administrative duties, and Mr. New was appointed the head administrator of IAIA. He preferred the title 'Director' to Superintendent, and this was approved. Not until 1967, six years after IAIA was established, and after five years of its operation, did Mr. New become its top responsible head. He is, in fact, the third — not the first — to be *overall* Director. The use of this term has been misleading.

12. The Indian Arts and Crafts Board has only been an advisory body, not an operational agency, other than operating several Indian museums, such as in Oklahoma and Dakota. It has always been detached from any authority over any of BIA's operations.

The old Indian School at Santa Fe had long since served its original purpose, in as much as many pupils were attending schools closer to their homes, on a day basis, or going to public schools. The BIA selected the Santa Fe plant as the best use and location for an Indian arts school, as the result of commercial trader interests and Indian art patrons — to meet changing times and belated recognition of certain unmet Indian youth needs.

May I add an additional comment?

The operation of the initial IAIA program was on a highly cooperative relationship by the staffs of all the departments and between the Institute and the Washington office of the Bureau of Indian Affairs. And in establishing an initial policy of seeking key persons of established success, preferably of Indian ancestries, among the first dozen IAIA employees to be recruited included the following. All were associates of longstanding. All came from the staff of Intermountain Indian School in Utah, except for Alvin Warren, Sr., who served in the IAIA staff the year prior to actual enrollment of students.

a. Alvin Warren, Sr. (Oneida), Director of Tribal and Public Relations. He has now retired.

b. Mrs. David (Mary) Stewart (Choctaw), still serving as Secretary.

c. Mr. David Stewart (Crow), Property and Procurement.

d. Miss Wilma Victor (Choctaw), Academic Director, now Special Assistant to Secretary of the Interior, Rogers Morton.

e. Miss Oleta Merry (Choctaw), Director of Guidance and Home-Living. She is now retired and my wife.

f. Allan Houser (Apache), Instructor of painting and sculpture.

g. Mrs. Allan (Ann) Houser (Navajo), Academic Secretary, still serving.

All of these persons were extremely competent in their respective fields and highly influential in setting the total tone of the Institute at its outset. All merit recognition. Some non-Indians were added.

In conclusion, I don't hold that these errors are your fault. But don't you think it is time for the facts to be told straight forwardly and correctly?

Cordially

George A. Boyce

Such misunderstandings about a school's beginnings would be trivial to students in most instances. In this instance, however, it greatly affected the students', as well as staff's, and public's perception of the school's program. At all times, Dr. Boyce publically made it clear that the curriculum he and his staff had developed had as its purpose the development of the whole individual. Instruction in the arts was to be used as a tool in this developmental process. One of Boyce's repeated sayings to his friends and colleagues was that given a well-rounded education, the Indian student who wished to become an artist "would find his art."[3]

Some staff and some students were disappointed to discover after committing themselves to the program that the IAIA under Boyce was not a school devoted exclusively to the arts but was structured in a highly academic manner to encourage both the high school and post-high graduates to seek further training in non-arts as well as arts-related fields. The bringing together of many tribes and many cultural traditions was carefully planned by Boyce and his advisors as an educational tool to help the student to understand his/her own culture, and to foster an appreciation of the cultures of others. Boyce was not a visual artist or an arts educator. He was however, a respected educator of Indian youth, a program builder, administrator, and creative writer. It was for these skills that he was chosen to initiate and lead the IAIA program, and it was primarily from this orientation that he built the curriculum.

The Rockefeller Foundation had funded over three summers, beginning in 1960, a program at the University of Arizona called The Southwest Indian Art Project. Lloyd New had been a co-director and facilitator in this program.

The program's purpose was to bring together practicing Indian artists, principally from reservations and unschooled, to expose them to a wide variety of cultural experiences, and to acquaint them with contemporary styles and trends in a wide spectrum of the arts, while encouraging them to retain aspects of their rich cultural traditions in their art works. Free housing, a studio, all materials, and ready access to all the resources of the University and community were put at the disposal of each participant. The hoped for end product of these intense and highly stimulating and encouraging experiences was a new body of art produced by Indians.

Although, as Boyce has said and Thompson has concurred, the art program first at the old SFIS and then at the IAIA was not originally prompted by the Rockefeller experiment, nevertheless, the influences of these workshops was felt from the first in the Institute curriculum through works being produced and disseminated by its participants and through the influence of staff members at the Institute who had led or participated in these summer sessions. Boyce had, in fact, sought New out, first as an arts consultant to the Institute and then as Arts Director because of New's various teaching and craft production experiences in Arizona and his affiliation with the Rockefeller workshops.

In the early days of the Institute, Boyce and New, working closely together, fused their backgrounds and philosophies into a highly workable curriculum. Although New became the Director of the Institute in 1967, the program remained, until the early seventies, very much as he and other staff members had formed it under Boyce's direction.

From the moment of his arrival in Santa Fe in the summer of 1961, George Boyce found himself at the center of a boiling controversy. The All-Indian Pueblo Agency did not intend to give in easily to the change in direction for the Santa Fe Indian School campus. They had made one concession two years earlier in cooperating with the small all-tribal art program which took place on their campus, but they were not prepared for the complete relinquishment of what they considered to be their school. Boyce's first two years in Santa Fe were as much taken up with defending the bureau's decision as with planning and setting in motion the new school's program. The SFIS and its staff, which over the years had slipped into routine and anonymity, regained its energy in a media fight that put the Institute concept in jeopardy for more than a year. Not since Chester Faris and the early thirties had the Santa Fe campus experienced such a man of purpose as Dr. George Boyce, and it was he who stood strongly against the outcries of opponents and critics until the Institute was an established fact.

Boyce had come to Santa Fe well prepared for such a task. He was a veteran of twenty-eight years of service in the Bureau and seventeen years service in public and private schools in the Eastern states. His tenure with the Bureau spanned the leadership of six BIA commissioners, from John Collier to Robert L. Bennett.

Born in Scranton, Pennsylvania in 1898, Boyce took his degrees at Trinity College in Connecticut, and at Cornell and Columbia Universities in New York, where he received his doctorate from Columbia Teacher's College in 1941. Boyce first entered the BIA in 1938 when he accepted a position as a curriculum specialist. His first assignment, as part of the Bureau's proposed implementation of the Meriam Report recommendations to make education relevant to Indian needs, was to survey educational needs of Indians throughout the country. For two and one-half years he traveled by camper bus, out of Kansas City, from reservation to reservation making contact with tribes, studying their history, talking with missionaries, traders, and others who lived among the Indians, attempting to discover the educational needs of the various tribes and discern approaches to their educational needs which would be the most relevant. As a result of this activity he was next appointed Director of Navajo and Hopi schools at Window Rock, Arizona, a post which he held for eight years. After his duty in Arizona he was engaged as a curriculum specialist and textbook writer for the BIA at Haskell Institute in Kansas, and as an Indian education specialist in Washington, D.C. In 1949 he was appointed as the first general superintendent of Intermountain School, Brigham City, Utah, the largest boarding school for Indians in the nation. It was while he was engaged in the training of Intermountain's 2300 students that he became involved, as his letter states, in the planning for a totally new approach to Indian education.

The first art program initiated at the old SFIS as a result of the

Emmons-Thompson meeting in Washington was quite small. The funds that were set aside for it allowed the hiring of only four instructors, who taught classes in silversmithing, painting, and ceramics to an enrollment of between twenty and thirty students. The staff was a carryover from the Studio group at the SFIS and included Geronima Cruz Montoya. The program was very little different from the old Studio program except that the art students, all eighteen or over, were separated from the academic program which served only grades one through nine. The SFIS was populated with approximately four hundred elementary students at that time, predominantly Apache and Navajo, with fewer than twenty Pueblo students in residence.

To be allowed to attend the SFIS in the late fifties and early sixties a student had to be certified to be a problem child, without parents, or from a broken home. As Boyce stated, the school was kept in operation "only by rounding up welfare or 'problem' children, for there were day schools, public schools, or boarding schools much closer to their homes. As this had been the accepted enrollment situation in the general academic program at the SFIS for some time, Bureau officials and Boyce were quite unprepared for the outcry that came from the Pueblo peoples during 1961-62.

The controversy seems to have begun when faculty at the old school, led by Geronima Cruz Montoya, contacted the press, New Mexico legislators, and President John F. Kennedy, protesting the change in direction for the school. It was determined by BIA officials that the teachers then employed at the SFIS were not suited to or qualified to instruct in the proposed specialized program.

Although the teachers had been offered transfers to other areas, they did not wish to go. Martin Vigil, president of the All-Pueblo Council, quickly took up their fight, claiming that the Pueblo Indians hadn't been informed of the new direction of the campus. What was really needed, stated Vigil, was a "Pueblo High School and Vocational School" in Santa Fe. He protested the "elitism" of catering to students interested only in the arts and further claimed that to train students in the arts was not suitable vocational training since "very few can make a living at it." New Mexico legislators, led by Sen. Dennis Chavez of Rio Arriba County, quickly jumped to the Pueblos' defense, and called for an investigation to be made of the proposed school, "all the way from Hildegard Thompson, the United Pueblo Agency, and the Gallup area, down to Mr. Autocrat himself, Dr. Boyce."

To the amazement and consternation of those working against the Institute concept, the Navajo nation came out publicly and solidly, in the *Navajo Times*, for the establishment of the IAIA saying, "We'll take a good long look after the program gets underway, and in the meantime, wish it every success."

So many rumors, complaints, accusations, and suppositions took place in the media during these two years that many old friends of the SFIS were drawn into the fight and publicly took sides. Oliver La Farge, long a friend of the Indian arts, wrote a historical article for the *New Mexican*, looking back at the accomplishments of the SFIS and adopting a "let's give it a chance" attitude toward the Institute. Olive Rush, a long-time friend of Dorothy Dunn and the Pueblo peoples, came out bitterly against the concept. Dunn, feeling compelled to take a public stand, commanded the attention of the Santa Fe community with a headline in the August 28, 1962 *New Mexican* which stated: "Dorothy Dunn Favors Arts for Indian Institute Here." The Santa Fe *New Mexican* also came out solidly for the IAIA in an editorial dated August 7, 1962.

Perhaps Martin Vigil's assessment that "very few can make a living at art" came about as a result of observing that the old Studio, Pueblo-dominated art was no longer held in popular demand and that his people would have to seek other forms of "vocational training." The old SFIS, from 1930 on, had built its program around the arts of the Studio as vocational training. When Studio painting began to slip in popularity, it was art that was blamed, not the kind of art. These ironies didn't escape Boyce, Thompson, or Phileo Nash, Commissioner of Indian Affairs, and each of them took a bold and vocal defense stand on the Institute concept in open Santa Fe meetings.

The Institute, as it was eventually established by Thompson, combined the emphasis on college preparatory curriculum and vocational training in the arts which she felt was relevant to meeting the students' needs. The Institute was an expression of Thompson's educational philosophy and as such was her pet project. Upon her retirement from the Bureau, she referred to herself as "the grandmother of IAIA."

Boyce's patience with his critics broke publicly in a *New Mexican* article of August 5, 1962, entitled "Boyce Shoots Back," when he summed up his feelings in the opening paragraph:

> Opposition to the program [at the IAIA] is vociferous and well-organized, but for the most part, criticism is inappropriate, misinformed, and inapplicable.

Clearly no one was prepared to admit defeat in this ideological battle. In the end it was the Bureau of Indian Affairs which quietly ended the debate by announcing the opening of the IAIA, as planned, for October 1, 1962. The *New Mexican*, anticipating this inevitable move, had begun to publish letters from students who wished to attend the Institute. These letters were filled with hope and anticipation. One such letter from Douglas Crowder, a Mississippi Choctaw from Ardmore, Oklahoma, more simply and sincerely expressed the pro-Institute philosophy than anyone had previously, when he wrote:

> I know there are relocation and trade schools but by all means I don't intend to be a factory worker because I can use art talent to be among the leaders instead of being led.

From Donna Mae Whitewing, Winnebago-Sioux, Winnebago, Nebraska, this letter came to the Institute:

> I know we have a place in society. Some of us must find it. Through your school and with the advancement of my talents I believe I can find my place in the world, and in doing so encouarge others to do the same.

The students, the last to have a voice, heard of the Institute in a diversity of unorganized ways and prepared to come, one hundred and forty-three in number, from nineteen states of the Union. The Pueblo Indians' strong objections to the program would not die, nor would other detractors cease to make their voices heard, but for these students a long awaited experiment had begun.

Although Boyce first arrived at the Santa Fe campus in the summer of 1961, the school plant was not to be handed over to the Institute until July 1, 1962. In the meantime, the old Santa Fe Indian School, with its small, newly formed art department, continued in operation. By October of 1961 the Bureau had approved Boyce's plans to tear down seven buildings, five of them dating from 1890, and had approved plans to build three new ones. The implementation of these plans, however, had to wait until the following summer. Meantime Boyce began the hiring of staff and the setting of curriculum goals and objectives. Mary Stewart, Dr. Boyce's secretary at Intermountain, transferred to the Santa Fe campus. She set up temporary offices in the living room of the old Employee's Club and began assisting Dr. Boyce in personnel recruitment and other preparations.

In selecting staff, Boyce deliberately sought not only "highly successful people," but "those of Indian ancestry." "Some 59 out of 81 employees hired in the first year of operation were Indians," a factor which "gave strength to the program from the beginning," said Boyce. Oliver Warren, of Oneida ancestry, who had assisted Boyce a year earlier in the Washington, D.C. planning, was appointed Director of Tribal and Public Relations and "served in initial recruitment of IAIA students." Wilma Victor, of Choctaw ancestry, who had headed one of the academic departments at Intermountain, was appointed academic Director. Another Intermountain employee, Oleta Merry, also of Choctaw ancestry, was appointed Director of Guidance and "was made responsible for directing home-living and community experience, social adjustment, and behavioral education." Lloyd New, known as Lloyd Kiva in his textile business in Arizona, "accepted a contract to draw up some general recommendations for an arts program." As a result of this paid consultancy, New was considered for the position of Arts Director.

Boyce wished to hire art instructors who were "producing artists with a high degree of recognized national reputation," for they would "keep up their contacts with the market, with style, economics, changes in fashion, and many other insights of importance in their vocation." By fall, Boyce had succeeded in finding several people who fulfilled his requirements. Among those hired were Charles Loloma, a Hopi, "nationally recognized for almost unsurpassable talent in design and technique in the field of various metals and ceramics," who was "exceptional in approaching problems of design through Indian traditions, while at the same time innovating departures for contemporary use"; Otollie Loloma, his wife, a Native American ceramist; Ralph A. Pardington, a ceramics graduate of Cranbrook Academy; Jim McGrath, an arts and crafts specialist; Allan Houser, renowned Apache painter and sculptor who had been teaching at Intermountain; and Louis Ballard, a musician of Osage-Quapaw ancestry to be appointed the Performing Arts Director. Miss Mary Mitchell, whom Boyce had recommended earlier to head the small art department at the SFIS was not hired as she was determined not to be a producing artist.

For the academic staff Boyce appointed Wilma Victor Principal of the grades ten-fourteen; Maryree Malone, home economics; Ester B. Smith, history; Alice Ramirez, library; Louis Rodriguez, counselor; John H. Maes, Jr., biology; Pablo Lopez, mathematics; Harvey Pommer, business education; and Monte LaBarge, science and math. Boyce also appointed an elementary staff for the displaced Navajo and Apache students who shared the campus with the Institute from 1962 to 1963, while their schools were being completed on their home reservations. Those appointed were; Wilma Victor, principal, Freda Austin, ninth grade; Geronima Cruz Montoya, elementary arts and crafts; Linda C. Love, fourth grade; M.O. Herrera, eighth grade; Joseph F. Maes, Jr., seventh grade; Estaven Zamora, fifth and sixth grades; and H.O. Hanson, seventh grade.

With the exception of Geronima Cruz Montoya, all personnel of the academic programs were non-Indians and of necessity chosen from the ranks of available teachers in their specialized areas as designated by Civil Service regulations. It should also be noted that the Civil Service ranking system accommodates only elementary and secondary teachers. Those teaching in the Institute program could be over-qualified for, but need not exceed the qualifications for a secondary teacher. In the cases of the Lolomas and Houser, who had no four-year degrees, exceptions were made to accommodate them as crafts or "training technicians" instructors.

This kind of rigidity in the Civil Service regulations caused difficulties for administrators attempting to staff a junior college-level, highly specialized curriculum with persons only minimally qualified to be secondary teachers. The Civil Service system also did not adequately address professional development and as a consequence, arts instructors working eight-hour days, as required by the Bureau, found the pursuance of their own work difficult, although required.

Boyce's experience and educational philosophy were challenged immediately by the planning for a new physical environment, fulfilling recruitment objectives he had set, curriculum development, and developing a plan for student supervision and enrichment for non-classroom hours. Boyce's approach during this critical period combined emphases on efficiency, fitting functions to needs, the Protestant work ethic, and his concepts of cultural pluralism. At all times he conveyed a sense of rigorous faith in his ideas.

Dr. Boyce conceived of the Indian artist as one who could make a unique contribution to American society. His art would contain reflections of his Indian heritage, a quality impossible for a non-Indian to achieve. Boyce believed that, historically, Indian cultures contained the roots of all arts — architecture, ceramics, painting, sculpture, and the performing arts. Because of this historical heritage, no field of art was to be barred to Indians on the grounds that a specific art form was not practiced within a given contemporary Indian culture. On the other hand, he also believed that Indians did not exist in a cultural vacuum. Students at the Institute were not to be limited to "traditional" arts. Since they partook of the larger society, as well as of their own cultures, they were to be encouraged to use all media, new techniques, and non-Indian art forms. The arts program at the IAIA was developed on the basis of these views, which were shared as well by Lloyd New, newly appointed Art Director.

Boyce was deeply concerned that the Institute prepare students to earn their livelihood, not merely a subsistence income, but one which would guarantee them a good standard of living. He felt that many students would have low aspirations unless they were otherwise conditioned. He conceived of an environmental pattern which would develop "wants" or "needs" in the students, an awareness and appreciation of material things not necessarily familiar to them in their pre-Institute days. Many of the physical innovations at the school, not found at other BIA schools, and the social customs he established there, were due to his great regard for environmental influences.

With an eye to enhancing school atmosphere and to creating "needs," well-designed furniture, rather than just functional institutional pieces, were purchased for living and dining areas. Family-style eating replaced institutional cafeteria lines and mess tables to help create a warm social mood. When the budget allowed, such "exotic" foods as strawberries were served. In the dormitory area, students were encouraged to decorate their rooms. To further a sense of space and individuality, the usual BIA bunk beds were dispensed with and replaced by single beds. Innovations such as those just described caused visiting BIA authorities to comment, "This place smells of money." In Boyce's view, however, these evaluations were from persons who "had too long become accustomed to and accepted as a standard, underfinancing with its consequent mediocre and unimaginative personnel, lack of necessary equipment, and depression buildings."

Indian culture and history were stressed in both academic and art courses. It was assumed, however, that as artists, future graduates would find it necessary to deal with all types of people in the process of promoting and selling their work. Whenever possible, therefore, attempts were made to familiarize the students with what might otherwise be strange social situations. To this end, Sunday dinners were formal affairs at which formal attire was expected. Arrangements were also made for students to dine with non-Indian families off-campus so that they might observe various family lifestyles.

The Institute officially opened for classes October 1, 1962.

Entry requirements stipulated that students be at least one-quarter Indian blood and members of a federally recognized tribe. Quotas, based on tribal population, determined the number of students accepted from each tribe. Applicants were to have high aptitudes in one of the arts and were requested to submit samples of their work. The age range was such as to allow entry to anyone fifteen to twenty-two years of age. Students in grades ten, eleven and twelve pursued an academic course leading to a high school diploma with electives in fine arts, crafts, and the performing arts. The two-year post-secondary program consisted of art training, college or technical/vocational school preparation, and college courses to be taken at colleges in the Santa Fe area.

Demolition of the old buildings and the construction of new ones had not gotten underway until July 1, 1962, the date set for transfer of authority from the SFIS to IAIA. A primary administrative concern in the fall of 1962 was the necessity of operating within an unfinished physical plant. As the academic building and several of the art studio buildings were still unready for occupancy, classes were started in temporary rooms and studios. Another negative physical factor was the overcrowding in the dormitories. By November, the delay in getting into classrooms and studios was resulting in "mounting tension," reported Boyce. It was not possible to begin weaving classes and there was as yet no group meeting place for the art students. Boyce reported to the area BIA office that students were beginning to feel "that these delays were diluting what they might get out of being here this year."

The Institute's program did attract students mentally and physically prepared to engage in a rigorous routine of academic and studio arts training, but it also soon became a multi-tribal dumping ground for young persons whose mental, physical, and attitudinal problems had become unsolvable on their home reservations. If the tribal authorities noted the student's interest in art, then the Institute was considered as a means of therapy for the student who lacked other available treatment. Boyce accused the tribal counselors of deliberately steering students away from the Institute program who were studious in nature or interested in sports. Careful screening of the applicants took place after this situation became apparent, but still few were turned away as Boyce's staff expressed a belief that they could assist these students. In many instances this proved to be the case. In other cases, however, all that could be done, after a series of reported difficulties, was to send the student back home.

Setting up an arduous schedule, Boyce and his wife visited the reservation homes of many troubled students in an attempt to assess the problems in the home environment so as to offer the students the sort of on-campus environment that would contribute to their development and treatment.

Boyce and his staff prepared in 1962 a twenty-page document entitled, *The IAIA, A Basic Statement of Purpose*, which was mimeographed and distributed to all staff and prospective students. This document was revised in May of 1963 and again in February of 1964. In July of 1963, Boyce produced a sixty-eight page *Guidebook to the IAIA*, and in August of 1965, he published a thirty-seven page document for the students entitled, *Learning and Living at the IAIA*.

These documents, submitted to the Bureau and contained in Boyce's files, clearly define the curriculum, campus life, and the relatedness of training in vocational/technical areas or arts areas. These documents also clearly address themselves to the education and care of the whole person as student at the IAIA. Dormitory living and personal relationships among students are addressed with the same importance as required curriculum.

Boyce's approach, based on his many years of surveying Indian educational needs stemming from the students' home environmental factors, greatly emphasized order, discipline, respect for and contribution to environment, a deep respect for one's own culture and the cultures of others, and the need for developing one's self beyond the student's years at the Institute. Boyce's philosophy, which was couched in the dominant belief of the sixties that given respect, caring, and a proper environment, one's life could be shaped in positive directions, exemplified the best that was available in Bureau philosophy. Boyce was at once benevolent, stern, concerned, paternalistic, self-righteous, stubborn, single-minded, idealistic, and determined that his philosophy would and could affect positive effects on those who accepted it and agreed to live by it.

The philosophical approach to the arts educational program was prepared by Lloyd New, Director of Arts, and states in part:

The art educational program of the Institute of American Indian Arts is based on the theory that traditional expressions in the arts by American Indians can be extended, commensurate to an effective evaluation of the demands of individuals and groups in terms of cultural needs. Indian art can be enriched in its present state by techniques that consider well the universal forces of creativity, contemporary demands, and respect for cultural difference. Indian art can be projected into the future by a willingness to consider the evolution of new forms, the adoption of new technological methods, and the fact that new incentives for expression by the individual must fill the void of inertia in Indian groups or tribal foces, in the rapidly changing Indian world.

No single approach to the individualistic requirements of the student body is possible. These students who are a part of a strong living tribal culture will be helped to express themselves in terms of the customs and manners of their group. Such expressions will be recognized as a group-type expression and may be expected to be less personally creative.

Correspondingly, the student who identifies as a member of a contemporary society, and whose identity is less "Indian" and who wishes to find himself as an artist of the world on a purely personal basis, will be encouraged to do so. In summary of this consideration, let it be said that the Institute will not expect homogeneity in the personalities of the student body, albeit they are all Indian. Each student will be helped to find *himself* as an artist with reference to his own identification.

Summarizing, the Institute will constantly work on the development of techniques for bringing through to the general stream of culture those unique qualities that Indian society has to offer. This will come about in an education program that looks not only at Indian culture, but can instill a realistic awareness of the general cultural milieu. The student must learn about the world in which he will function.

New's art philosophy encompasses almost five pages of this total report, laying the groundwork for the elective art classes for the high school and the arts curriculum for the post-secondary program. New, like Boyce, is a prolific writer and in this document, as in many others that followed, he would define and redefine the Institute's purpose.

The high school academic curriculum was set up in a similar fashion to that of other well-staffed American high schools of the sixties. Its ready availability of arts courses as electives was, however, exceptional. Standard texts for instruction were chosen from the Bureau or the State of New Mexico's education resources. The day was divided into eight periods, with art classes consisting of two periods. Extra academic activities were encouraged for after school hours. Post-secondary students (grades 13 and 14) might devote their day, but for the exception of two academic courses, to the study of the arts and cultural studies. Postgraduate students could also, if they chose, take any high school academic course they felt they needed in addition to their academic work at area schools.

As listed in the IAIA *Basic Statement of Purpose* publication the arts curriculum was quite comprehensive.

REQUIRED AND ELECTIVE ART SUBJECT FIELDS

I. *Aesthetic Survey of Indian Arts and Culture*
   (Required)

All students are exposed to three class periods weekly. The course explores Indian expression, historical and contemporary, North and South American continents, in areas of philosophy, literature, dance, costume, music, and visual arts.

II. *Elements of Design and Principles of Art*
    (Required)

All students study this course, branching out from a close look at design as used by Indians to design in the universal sense.

III. *Exploratory Experience*
     (Required)

All new students explore seven major art areas:

1. Music and Performing Arts
2. Painting
3. Sculpture
4. Ceramics
5. Textiles, woven and decorated
6. Jewelry and Metals
7. Creative Writing

IV. *Major Art Offerings*

1. Music and Performing Arts
2. Painting.
3. Sculpture
4. Ceramics
5. Textiles, woven and decorated
6. Jewelry and Metals
7. Creative Writing

V. *Types of Elective Art Courses*
   (Subject to modification according to student interests and administrative limitations)

Creative Writing
Introduction to Professional Writing
    Poetry
Exhibition Arts
    Museum and gallery techniques and
    sales display

Individual Instruction in Music
Instrumental
Music Theory I
    General music appreciation
    Harmony and melody
Music Theory II
    Harmony
    Counterpoint
    History of Msuic
V. *Types of Elective Art Courses*
Music Theory II (continued)
    Composition
Orchestra
General Music
Performing Arts
    Speech
    Drama
    Dance
    Stagecraft
Graphic Arts
    Block Printing
    Serigraphy
    Monoprinting
    Layout and lettering
The Artist in Business
    Business Principles
    Production
    Sales
    Advertising
    Promotion
Art in Education
Commercial Art
    Design and Layout
Architecture
    Pre-architecture
    Drafting
Portrait Painting
Traditional Indian Techniques
Fashion Techniques
Weaving
Printed Textiles
Ceramics

Pottery
Ceramic Sculpture
Metals
Jewelry
Holloware
Welded Metals
Sheet Metal Sculpture
Structural Sculpture

Scarcely had the Institute begun operation when it was reveiwed by Mamie L. Mizen, a member of the Senate Appropriations Committe. In her report she described the IAIA program in glowing terms, commenting particularly on the high quality of the arts faculty. Mizen's enthusiasm for the Institute seemed boundless. She concluded her lengthy and comprehensive report by saying, "Truly, the institute of American Indian Arts is one of the best things that the Federal Government has ever done for its Indian people."[4] Within the first three years of the Institute's operation, student achievement underscored the report's optimism.

The most comprehensive collection of American Indian paintings, sculpture, and handicrafts ever assembled was exhibited at the Department of Interior in the spring of 1964. Many entries were by IAIA students, among those were Larry Bird, Hank Gobin, and Elaine Rice. Some of the work had originally been designed by the students for the Miccosukee Tribal Center in Southwestern Florida. Institute work also appeared in the fall of 1965 at an exhibition of young Indian artists' work at the Riverside Museum of New York City. These works were also seen again in 1966 at the Department of Interior's Second Annual Invitational Exhibition of American Indian Paintings in Washington, D.C. Competing in a wide range of media, including creative writing, Institute students took many awards at the Fourth Annual Scottsdale National Indian Art Exhibition in the spring of 1964. Angelo John, a Navajo IAIA student, took first place in Art and in the Indian Arts and Crafts division at the 1965 Arizona State Fair.

In March of 1965, President Yameago, of the Republic of Upper Volta, made a state visit to the United States. Upon his expression of interest in American Indian art and culture, President Johnson invited Institute students to dance at the White House state dinner in honor of the African president. The following month, Institute students participated in the First American Indian Performing Arts Festival, held in Washington, D.C. The program entitled *Sipapu* was written, staged, and directed by Lloyd New, with assistance from

Roland Meinholtz, drama instructor, and Louis Ballard, Performing Arts Director at the Institute.

Mrs. Stewart Udall, wife of the Secretary of Interior, for a time was in charge of the Indian arts for the Interior Department and was the moving force for the Washington shows and performances.

The period of the early and middle sixties in the Institute's history can well be considered its "golden period." National and international attention were constantly focused on the school by articles in such prestigious publications as the *New York Times, The New Yorker, Life* and *Time* magazines, the *Washington Post, Christian Science Monitor,* and various foreign as well as regional and local publications. The Bureau touted the Institute through its own publications and news releases, promoting the school's program and the various shows sent out from its collection, both here and abroad. Faculty members such as Houser, Ballard, and Fritz Scholder garnered positive publicity for the school with their professional achievements and greatly influenced more students to come to Santa Fe. Vincent Price, President of the Arts and Crafts Board, focused a good deal of national media attention on the school. Price established the Vincent Price awards for creative writing at the Institute and also encouraged other authors to do so. A commercial film describing the school and its activities, narrated by Price, was made for national distribution, prompting TV stations to send crews to interview the Institute staff and film the program in progress. Edna Ferber often visited the school and read for the students. She also contribued money to the Performing Arts Department. Political figures, anxious to espouse ethnic causes, made frequent visits to the Institute, vying for opportunities to buy student work at the Hookstone Gallery on campus or to arrange student shows or performances in their areas.

The campus quickly became a lively place and the national center for the renewed interest in all things "Indian" as Americans began to take up the "ethnic cause" in the sixties, and adopted, in some instances attributes of Indian dress, Indian philosophies, and Indian thought along with the attributes of other minority cultures as they sought a broader understanding of American cultures long oppressed and ignored.

All of this attention put the Institute in good standing with the public, educators, and devotees of the Indian arts, but it only further fostered resentments and a feeling among Santa Fe area Indians that the Institute was an "elite" organization. They felt that the Institute was given too much freedom in its decision-making and funding processes and that much of this could be controlled if it were regionally instead of nationally governed and financed. There was a division among the faculty and staff and an uneasy feeling on campus that the Institute was perhaps being used for political aggrandizement by some persons. There was the fear that this new focus would destroy the original purpose of the Institute's educational program. Boyce believed that it was from the period of political patronage that the original purpose of the IAIA, as he had conceived it, began to alter and he predicted, well before his retirement in 1966, that the Institute's curriculum would take a new direction.

However tumultuous the early years were from an administrative or staff view, from some of the students' viewpoints these were happy and fulfilling times. The program had so quickly grown that by the fall of 1963, 278 students were enrolled. By 1964, 334 students were in residence, with these numbers levelling off in 1965 to 284 and in 1966 to 260. The co-educational enrollment was male dominated and never represented less than 25 states. Most of the students commenting on their program in the early and mid-sixties reported that the excitement of spending each day in learning more about their own cultures and the cultures of others was of primary importance to them.

The works produced at the IAIA were very much influenced by the quality and personality of the teacher. In such a familial setting, students gathered around the teacher or teachers of their choice and oftentimes closely emulated their work. But by the same token some instructors were very much influenced by the works of certain of their students, and all the students greatly affected each other.

In the early days of the Institute, many of the faculty and staff lived in campus housing, making an exchange of ongoing communication even more accessible than at most boarding schools.

Hank Gobin, former Arts Director at the Institute and past student of the IAIA and SFIS art program of 1960, says there was "no one kind of art that could be labelled the Institute style." "Indeed," says Gobin, "there is no one kind of art done by Indians who attended the school that could be called an Indian style or movement. The artist of Indian heritage finds himself, as all artists, expressing the sum of his life's experiences."

On the rosters of these early years at the Institute are found such names as T.C. Cannon (now deceased), Doug Hyde, Bill Sousa, Kevin Red Star, Earl Eder and Earl Biss. Each depicts elements of his own heritage in his work as distilled through a wide variety of past and contemporary art idioms, and each has developed a distinctive and easily identifiable style and subject matter range. All lived most of the time in the Santa Fe area, staying in close touch with each other, and supporting the others' efforts. Other students from the period, having gone on to receive further training, returned to be staff or faculty members at the IAIA. This series of events early on prompted observers to draw parallels with the events surrounding the SFIS and the thirties. If this process caused "a school of American Indian art" to build up in Santa Fe in the thirties, then this must be a "new school of American Indian art" building itself up around the IAIA, they concluded. It is a judgement that has persisted and has become part of the prevailing mythology surrounding the Institute's beginnings.

It would be more accurate to say that the work produced at the Institute in the early years was experimental, eclectic, and unselfconsciously naive. As a critic for *Arts Magazine*, who attended the Riverside Museum's showing the works of "Young American Indian Artists," said in 1966:

> Whereas our artists have consciously explored new expressive modes in the exotic arts of Africa and the Orient, the young American Indian, using elements of his own heritage and found objects from the reservation, creates with but an introduction to oil painting works immediately suggestive of our most modern art. It is difficult to disassociate the works of Kirby Feathers from Jackson Pollock, or Kevin Red Star from Motherwell, or Zackery Toahty from Georgia O'Keeffe, or Tommy Montoya from Leger or current Pop Artists.[5]

Although Boyce, during his last year on campus, found his directorship usurped many times by direction from Washington, he continued to assess the program and plan for its future. He saw himself at war with opposing viewpoints. His, he said, was the war to protect the "Indian's right to be different."

He began to plan and requested funds for a much more extensive recruiting program. He feared that cutbacks in funding in the school's budget, which began as early as 1964, would seriously impair the school's offerings and he and is staff met to assess the effects of these cuts and propose alternatives to strengthen the curriculum. The Vietnam war years were beginning to take their toll on the budget of the Department of Interior, and the Bureau-designated regional funding process forced area schools to vie for program funding. Although Boyce proposed funds and facilities for an eventual 500 students per year by the year 1975, enrollment would never again be as high at the Institute as it was in its earliest years. Rigid funding procedures, an inflexible civil service system, cutbacks of programs to fit needs to funds available, and the constant seesawing of the programs offered after 1970, would gradually decrease, not increase, the IAIA's enrollment.

Boyce continued to the very last to attempt to strengthen the academic and guidance faculty as he observed that the students who appeared the most interested in attending the Institute were those of high creative nature, above national norms in intelligence, but who greatly lacked skills in the English language and in social adaptation. Boyce felt that students in the early years had turned more dramatically to the arts in their curricular preference, not only because of their interest in the arts, but because their academic classes and dormitory routines were unchallenging. He continued to propose to Bureau officials and all who would listen, that to make such a program as the IAIA's workable, creative and innovative approaches must be found to actively engage the student in all aspects of academic life.

Announcing his plans for an early retirement in 1966, Boyce set about putting things in order for the fall session. When asked by Secretary Udall as to what sort of person he thought should be his successor, Boyce replied that, "that depended on the kind of school that Udall was proposing that the Institute would become."

In June, Boyce gathered his staff together and they jointly wrote a proposal to Udall, depicting the qualifications necessary to fulfilling the post. Shortly after, Howard Mackey, Director of the Academic Program, was appointed as an interim acting-superintendent by Bureau officials.

Boyce retired to his private life: his writing, lecturing, and political activity in Santa Fe. Upon his retirement, an exhibit of works produced during his superintendancy was hung at the IAIA, and notables from throughout the country attended the reception or sent messages to be read in his honor.

In May of 1967, Acting-Superintendent Mackey, with the assistance of the Institute's administrative manager, W.W. Larson, assembled one of the most comprehensive documents ever put together concerning the Institute. Entitled, *The Institute of American Indian Arts, A Program Memorandum*, it outlined the history, curriculum, fiscal history, student statistics, and program recommendations for the years 1962-67. To Boyce's recommendations of the previous year were added further recommendations for reduction in student body, reduction in faculty and staff, and elimination of some arts and acadmic programs. Mackey warned the Department of Interior administrators that unless a solution was found to the gradual lessening of fiscal resources, "the inevitable rise in the per capita cost will ultimately destroy the whole Institute program."

Mackey proposed that a separate arts vocational school be set up on campus, where those not suited to the present program could be taught in an apprenticeship manner the kind of skills that would produce students proficient in production, sales, and marketing of their own products and the products of others.

Such a recommendation is surprising in view of the fact that arts staff was being cut, along with facilities and supplies. Such a project may have gained regional support, and as such, could have garnered additional regional funding. One can only speculate that this may have been a motivating factor for such a proposal; however, the proposal was not funded.

After one year of supervising the program, both Mackey and Larson asked to be transferred; Mackey to a post in Roswell, New Mexico, and Larson to a post in Samoa. Robert L. Bennett, Commissioner of Indian Affairs, himself an Indian, appointed Lloyd New, of Cherokee ancestry, the next administration head of the IAIA. New, designated to take up his duties in the fall term of 1967, broke the tradition of being labelled Superintendent and chose to be called Director instead.

U.S. Indian School, ca. 1895

Ramona Indian School

U.S. Indian School, ca. 1900-05

U.S. Indian School

St. Catherine's Indian School, 1912

Carpentry class, U.S. Indian School, 1904

*Whiting Hall, New West Academy, Ladd's
University of New Mexico, Santa Fe, NM*

Classroom, U.S. Indian School, 1900

Student murals, U.S. Indian School, 1930's

Arts and Crafts Building, U.S. Indian School, 1932

Cafeteria, U.S. Indian School, ca. 1935

"The Drummers" by Leo Proctor and Doug Crowder

Pottery class with Maria Martinez, ca. 1935

IV
THE INSTITUTE OF AMERICAN INDIAN ARTS 1970-1978

I did what I felt was right in terms of what made common sense. (Lloyd New, Director of the Institute of American Indian Arts, Santa Fe, New Mexico, May 6, 1977)

Lloyd New, of Cherokee ancestry, was appointed by Commissioner Robert L. Bennett, an Oneida Indian, to head the Institute of American Indian Arts (IAIA) in the summer of 1967. New's directorship at the Institute would span an era of renewed interest in the Indian life, encompassing such diverse elements as the confrontation at Wounded Knee, the Kennedy Senate hearings on Indian education, the formation of the *American Indian Movement* (AIM) and its struggle for change, the Indian Self Determination Act, and, the rededication of the Indian Preference Act. New's tenure at the IAIA from 1967-1978 would also encompass some of the most tumultuous of times in Indian politics and some of the most forward thinking of times in Bureau education. His was a most challenging and difficult directorship, spanning the wide educational philosophical differences from the culture-sensitive benevolent paternalism of Boyce's era to the unexpected effects of tribal self-determination on the Institute's national program. Only a man well-prepared to meet such a diversity of challenges could have met those that New would have to face head-on for more than a decade.

New was born in Fairland, Oklahoma in 1916. He was educated at Oklahoma State University, the Art Institute of Chicago, and the University of New Mexico, receiving his bachelor's degree in art education from the University of Chicago in 1938. He studied at the Laboratory of Anthropology in Santa Fe, New Mexico in 1939. Leaving Santa Fe late in 1939, he took a position as instructor in arts and crafts at the U.S. Indian school in Phoenix, Arizona, where he also ran a small gallery. In the summer of 1941 he conducted, for his own information, an arts and crafts survey in Mexico. For the next four years New served in the military.

Returning to Scottsdale in 1945, New, with his artist wife and two Navajo leather workers, began what was to become the Lloyd Kiva Studios and Crafts Center. The studios quickly expanded into an architectural compound housing twenty-five Indian craftspersons, working in their own crafts specialty. New and the group that he had brought together produced leather goods, textiles, clothing, jewlery in gold and silver, and many other items based on traditional techniques and materials styled in a contemporary manner. During the summers while administering the Crafts Center, New served as an instructor in art education to the teachers of Indian schools in Carson City, Nevada (1949), Santa Fe and Salem, Oregon (1950), and Brigham City, Utah (1951). In 1959 he became co-director of the Southwest Indian Arts Project at the University of Arizona, where he conducted these summer workshops through 1961.

In 1961, before accepting his post as Arts Director of the IAIA, New went on a survey tour to study cultural and socio-economic conditions in Peru, Ecuador, and Columbia with some time spent in Panama, Guatemala, the Yucatan, and Mexico City. That same year he was appointed by Commissioner Nash as Secretary of the Indian Arts and Crafts Board. A textile artist and painter, as well as arts educator, New continued to be honored by membership and participation in various arts, crafts, and design organizations in the U.S., Canada, and abroad. A prolific writer on cultural and ethnic education, New frequently delivered papers and produced articles on these topics as well as on arts and crafts, several times being designated as the U.S. representative to World Crafts Conferences.

In 1978, after eleven years as director of the IAIA, New retired to private life to live in Santa Fe where he currently resides, remaining active in his own art work, as well as continuing to devote time to the Institute in arranging for shows of student works outside Santa Fe, and has a number of written works in progress on various aspects of the Institute's program.

New's early years at the IAIA were plagued with the same difficulties as had been Boyce's lot. Gradually reduced or leveled financing, regionally directed funding, rigid Civil Service regulations, and poor relations with Pueblo leaders and tribal leaders throughout the U.S. continued, and despite his best efforts, intensified. The Guidance Department, a carry-over from the old SFIS, continued to be of almost daily concern, and although some arts and academic teachers who were not effective had voluntarily left or been released, filling their posts within the Civil Service guidelines did not greatly alleviate any of the earlier problems. The academic department continued to be the weakest link in the overall program, causing the students to further push themselves away from the academic side of the program to spend more and more time in the studios with the arts personnel.

The most severe problem, however, because it was outside the control of the IAIA personnel, was the continued referral of problem students to the program. The school administration found itself caught between attempting to tighten admission standards and the tribal opinion that the arts as therapy could benefit troublesome young tribal members. Fearing a further loss of potential students if tribes vetoed any aspect of the Institute's program, the administration was forced to gradually lessen rather than tighten admissions procedures. Admitting some students not suited to the program reinforced IAIA critics' views that as a whole the Institute students were a bad lot and further inhibited enrollment by tribes who feared that their young men and women would be caught up in alcohol, drugs, vandalism, and militarism if allowed to live on the IAIA campus. Thus the Institute had inherited more than the old SFIS campus, it had inherited its biggest problem as well.

However, to most educators and the general public, the IAIA in 1967 displayed only great hope for the futures of Indian youth and their cultural and artistic development. Emerson Blackhorse Mitchell, a Navajo student at the IAIA, and Mrs. T.D. Allen, his creative writing teacher, published a book in 1967 based on Mitchell's reservation and school life entitled, *Miracle Hill, The Story of A Navajo Boy*. This book, written by Mitchell in his unusual Anglicized vernacular, and carefully guided to publication by Mrs. Allen, brought the Institute renewed attention in the areas of creative writing.

Various shows of visual arts, which continued to be solicited from the Institute's collection, caused a continued flow of newspaper and magazine articles to be written praising the Institute program and analyzing the artistic efforts of the students. Since the Washington, D.C. performance of *Sipapu* the Institute had gained increased public interest from its performing arts as well.

In an interview with Santa Fe *New Mexican* reporter Vina Windes upon his appointment in August of 1967, Lloyd New restated his educational philosophy for the Institute, saying:

The greatest need of Indian youth today. . .is a sense of pride in heritage.

It's time we got busy trying to help them awaken to the same pride and spirit they had in the old days.

The Bureau of Indian Affairs (BIA) is beginning to realize this emphasis is needed. . .and I have every reason to believe they are ready to continue this philosophical approach.

America's whole history of dealing with the Indians since it decided to trade bullets for benevolence illustrates that programming for its wards has never been intelligently liked to the cultural strengths within their Indian identities.

The American Indian will never give up his identity. . .yet when we plan for educating them, we assume they must. We want to develop methods to teach the American Indian how to live in today's world, to belong and contribute to it, to take his rightful place in it.

Deplorable statistics. . .indicate Indians are apathetic; are not taking advantage of what's available to them. But while other minority groups are fighting to get out of the ghetto, the American Indian is fighting like crazy to maintain his identity as an Indian.

I believe it is possible for Indians to exist in 1967, or in 1977, and contribute [to] and enjoy their own identity, adding to the strengths in their own culture whatever new knowledge they need to exist in modern society.

Inevitably, this tribal structure is breaking down, leaving the individual high and dry. Indian teenagers today are not one with the group, as were their parents. They have to have the kind of education, therefore, that enables them to face life as an individual, to maintain whatever cultural identity they can without continuing the devastating breakdown of that culture, without giving it up wholesale.

[My] approach, mapped out in the school's [IAIA's] original prospectus, will be to provide the education to enable Indian youth to find self affirmation for what they are, as persons and artists, so that they can make value judgements regarding their own lives, free from the confusion surrounding minority groups generally, free from the confusion they have about themselves. [1]

In this interview, New further outlined some of the actions he hoped to take as Director. He was very concerned that the students at the IAIA hadn't been included as much as they could have been in planning their program saying, "We plan courses for kids, but we never ask the kids. We never give them credit for being capable of helping to plan the world we're making for them." He said further of the students that although they, "are generally below the normal achievement level [and] cannot go the normal education route. . . we're putting a large number into college; [and] they are making a tremendous impact on the art world." The key to New's hope for the school, a hope he had carried from its early years was that, "In time . . .the IAIA can create an institution — a sort of researching, living museum — which will put the Indian's background into perspective for him." This public statement set the tone for the sort of institution New would seek to build until his retirement from the Bureau.

The summary of the Institute's goals and objectives as previously noted under Boyce's administration were revised with little change in 1966, 1968, and 1970. The enrollment in the high school had stabilized at around 200 during these years, as had the post-secondary enrollment. All administrators since 1962 had hoped for and projected a combined enrollment of 500 in the high school and post-high school programs, but that was never attained. In fact, both gradually decreased in size after 1970 and the postgraduate program reached all-time lows after 1978 when the high school program was discontinued. To enhance the enrollment in the high school the ninth grade was added from 1969 to 1971.

When New's administration was set firmly in place he began to employ former students who had gone elsewhere for advanced degrees, in teaching and museum positions — a trend which he would be forced to develop further in the seventies under the constraints of the Indian Preference Act, and which would lead eventually to a familial inbreeding in the staffing pattern.

In June of 1967, Robert M. Coates, writer for the *New Yorker*, published a lengthy article on the Institute, focusing most of his attention on the art program and the art students' production and daily lives. Coates made a comparison between between the Institute and a number of schools he visited in Italy, run by the Quakers under the Union for the Fights Against Illiteracy (UNLA). At these schools, scattered among the poorer Italian villages, free instruction was offered to peasants and farmers, usually at night. Coates had sensed in Italy the same enthusiasm among the instructors and excitement among the students as he felt overwelmed by during his month at the IAIA. After Coates had attended a luncheon with the students at the Institute, which he discovered later was really a class given by the Guidance Department to teach table manners, polite conversation, public speaking, and "dating techniques," he noted a further parallel. The "people at UNLA were confronted with a special problem," he said. "What was the point of taking a peasant from a remote, locked-in hill village and teaching him to read and write if he was then to be returned to his tiny village and left there with no way of using his new talents?" "As a result," Coates said, "the UNLA program [was] expanded to include courses in a variety of crafts, such as plumbing, electrical work and mechanics." "In the case of the Indians," Coates concluded, "a corollary problem presented itself: What was the use of training young people the skills of applied and other arts if, because of their elementary behavior educations, they might only make fools of themselves in the world their training would lead them into?"[2]

Although Boyce, Mackey, and New would not have put the situation as bluntly, each firmly subscribed to strong literacy training, training in the social skills of the dominant culture, and vocational training at the IAIA or elsewhere that would assure the student of making a livelihood on or off the reservation.

Coates' observation was a timely one as the Institute, along with other schools of its kind throughout the world — schools which emphasized literacy training along with training in producing and merchandising the indigenous arts to a national and world market — joined together in the seventies under the United Nations Educational, Scientific, and Cultural Organization (UNESCO) in an International Association of Art so that they might better communicate their methods and products. Boyce, had hoped the IAIA could become a prototype for schools of this sort. He and members of his staff had written and presented papers in the early sixties proposing such organizations to be established in Mexico with ties to the IAIA.

But New, as Boyce before him, wished to go beyond these schools of segregated arts and enable the IAIA students, through a wide range of influence and activities, to perform as artists who were Indian, not as Indian artists. In doing so, both set for themselves a goal not previously reached in other such segregated situations. There was a difference in educational philosophy, however, between the two men in that Boyce saw the students' involvement in the arts principally as a means to an end, while New saw the arts as the end to which the students were to strive, thereby subtly redefining the Institute into an art school, rather than a school that employs the arts as a tool in the development of the individual.

Most significant to New's emerging educational philosophy were the Senate Subcommitte Hearings on Indian Education of 1968-1969, chaired first by Sen. Robert F. Kennedy, and after his death, by his brother Sen. Edward Kennedy. The final recommendations of this committee are contained in the report, *Indian Education: A National Tragedy—A National Challenge*. This report surveyed the whole of Indian education, focusing not on the past but on what was presently being done. Bureau boarding schools fared very badly in the report, as they had in 1928 with the *Meriam Report*. In fact, the Committee found in many areas of Bureau education that little had changed since the late twenties — only the numbers of students had increased.

The Committee states in part in its summary:

What concerned us most deeply, as we carried out our mandate, was the low quality of virtually every aspect of the schooling available to Indian children. The school buildings themselves; the course materials and books; the attitude of teachers and administrative personnel; the accessibility of school buildings — all these are of shocking quality.

The Committee developed statistics that indicated that:

The average educational level for all Indians under Federal supervision is 5 school years; more than one out of every five Indian men have less than 5 years of schooling; that the dropout rates for Indians are twice the national average; that academic supervisory positions in the Bureau had increased as much as 144 per cent since 1953 while teaching positions had increased 20 per cent; that only 18 per cent of students in Bureau schools go on to college (national average in 1969, 50%); that only 3 per cent of those who enroll in college graduate (national average, 32%); that the BIA spends $18 per year, per student on textbooks and supplies (national average, $40); and that only one of every 100 Indian college graduates will receive a masters degree.

Although the IAIA served students fourteen to twenty-two by bringing them hundreds and thousands of miles from their homes to an old renovated and partially temporary physical plant, it received high praise from the Committee for the thrust of its curriculum, its staffing, its attention to the individual and his/her culture, and the success rate of its programs when viewed in terms of graduates, college enrollees, and college graduates.

Many tribal leaders who were asked to speak at the Congressional hearings gave impassioned testimony as to the therapeutic value of the arts on young members of their tribes who were attending the Institute. Although they regretted young people having to travel so far from home to receive this sort of attention and training, the tribal leaders felt this disadvantage was outweighed by the benefits of the students being trained where their culture was held to be of great value. It was acknowledged that the Institute program had been an expensive one, but it had circumvented, through its expansive staffing and equipping, many of the shortcomings other boarding schools had been faulted for in the hearings. As its educational program was unique in the Bureau, it was held to be exemplary in many of its aspects.

In addressing the Institute's future, the committee suggested the following list of priorities:

a.   The most urgent need for the Institute is to get to the bottom of the language problem.

b . Physical Plant:
  1. Dormitory expansion should be considered
  2. Needs for an instructional media center
  3. Inadequate storage space
  4. Inadequate shop area
  5. New complex of art studios

c . The Institute be given financial support to continuing programs already begun in the development of literature music, drama, museum training and advanced training for graduates.

d . The Institute should be raised to the level of a four year college supported by the BIA.

The Institute has had considerable success in instilling a cultural pride in Indian students by providing them with opportunities for creative expression. The individual-oriented programs recognize the importance of a sense of identity. By becoming a college, the Institute could provide a college-wide curriculum for Indians which considers their culture and history—something unique in higher education. The valuable lessons learned and put into practice by the Institute should be expanded into a college curriculum so that the Institute might become a model for Colleges interested in developing innovative programs, such as in teacher training, which recognize Indian needs.

The interest focused on the Institute by the Senate Hearings would lead to two comprehensive evaluations of the IAIA—one conducted in 1970 by John C. Rainer, Executive Director of the Commission on Indian Affairs of New Mexico, and the second in 1971-72 by regional Bureau evaluators at the request of James C. Hawkins, Director of the Office of Education Programs, Washington, D.C. The focus of both of these reports was to test the feasibility of a four-year college to replace the post-secondary program.

Central to the planning was New's concept of a cultural center as he expressed it in 1967 upon his appointment. Implicit also was New's immerging belief that to create a school of art and cultural research, he must begin with an older, more mature student body, and these students would need more than two years of work to develop into professional artists. New had been encouraged in this concept by testimony and support at the Senate Hearings; all of which focused new attention on the potential of the Institute.

In 1969, as well, the U.S. Department of the Interior and the Indian Arts and Crafts Board published jointly a handsome 59-page booklet on the Institute's program entitled, *Native American Arts I.* The preface was written by Vincent Price, chairman of the Arts and

Crafts Board, and the philosophy statement, entitled *Cultural Differences as the Basis for Creative Education*, was written by Lloyd New originally as a position paper in 1964. This publication was widely distributed to colleges, universities, art schools, and secondary schools across the country. Ten thousand copies were ordered for the first printing. It was New's first opportunity to speak out for cultural education to a wide and varied audience.

New perceived that ideally the Institute was foremost an institution whose function it was to serve the Indian youth's cultural needs within an institutional framework. Secondly, it was a training ground for young aspiring artists and craftspersons where these needs could be determined and attended to. The goals and objectives of the 1970 IAIA program began to put this view of the Institute's function into perspective.

In 1970, the last year that an unbroken sequence of grades 9-14 would be offered along with the post-secondary program, the goals and objectives of the academic and arts programs shows a small but subtle shift toward the arts over the academic program in importance and the new emphasis on cultural studies.

Classes offered in 1970 varied from the 1966 revisions, the last major revisions, in the addition of business courses such as typing (I and II), business principles, office practice, business in art, clerical office practices, and Hookstone sales. Although Mackey's arts vocational school as a separate entity had not been funded, these courses were an attempt to partially fill the need for persons trained to merchandise their art or the art of others.

On April 9, 1970, Commissioner of Indian Affairs, Louis R. Bruce, the third Indian to hold this position, asked John C. Rainer, Taos Indian and Executive Director of the Commission on Indian Affairs for the State of New Mexico, to establish a committee composed of outstanding Indian leaders and nationally-known educators, to examine and evaluate the Institute and to determine whether the school was being administered and was functioning in an efficient manner to serve the needs of its several Indian constituencies. Rainer chose for the committee, Helen Peterson, Ogalala Sioux, Director of American Indian Development, Inc., Denver; Dr. Anne M. Smith, formerly curator of the Museum of New Mexico and an authority in the field of Indian education; Popovi Da, Indian artist and businessman; Dr. Frank M. Tippetts, Associate Professor of Art, Brigham Young University; Dr. James P. Shannon, Vice President of St. John's College, Santa Fe; and Tom Segundo, Chairman of the

Papago Tribal Council.

For five days the committee evaluated faculty, staff, and students. They reported that, "On the basis of these several interviews, the Committee has concluded that the IAIA, Santa Fe, New Mexico, has reached a critical point in its history." In a very detailed and thoughtful report, the Committee made nine administrative and curricular recommendations it felt were of urgent importance to be acted upon.

The Transition Team of Evaluators, led by John W. Tippeconnie, Jr., BIA Education Specialist, from the Indian Resources Center in Albuquerque, upon surveying the IAIA program in October of 1972, would conclude that of the Rainer report nine recommendations, only one had been fully acted upon even through the conclusions of the Transition Report group closely paralleled those of the earlier team. Rainer's group had suggested "phasing out grades nine and ten in an orderly fashion." This had been accomplished as suggested in successive years 1971 and 1972.

In 1972, Gene Leuka, Bureau Education Specialist, did a follow up on Rainer's report. He found that the impetus created by the Transition evaluation in that same year on the IAIA campus, caused some of the Rainer recommendations to have begun to be effected. Most encouraging to Leuka was the preparation of some special teaching materials for IAIA staff, filmmaking which had been established in the art program, and administrative plans for in-service training for teachers of Indian children. Leuka felt that the Rainer recommendations for a four-year college at IAIA, having a cultural orientation, was premature until Institute personnel proved that they could create programs and materials at least as exciting and effective as colleges and universities were producing throughout the country in their Indian Studies programs.

At the very time that New's educational philosophy for the IAIA was being widely disseminated through national Bureau and independent publications, and there was high enthusiasm rising on the part of some of the faculty and staff for the four-year, art college concept, regional Bureau opinion was questioning anew the Institute's very existence. Regional adversaries of the Institute found this possible, as much of the local and regional publicity which had surrounded the IAIA's daily efforts had cooled by the time of Commissioner Bruce's administration (1969-1973). The faculty and staff, long secure in the roles they played in the Institute's beginnings, had settled into a comfortable routine, and although many shows of the visual arts and some performing arts were requested and sent out from the IAIA, these events seemed to be expected and passed large-ly unnoticed in the regional press. A second generation faculty, IAIA-trained, had become an established part of the program in the arts division, outnumbering the senior faculty members at times. The publicity and public attention of the seventies was not strong enough or sustained enough to throw up a wall of invulnerability around the school's mode of operation. The publicity that did emanate from the school was policy-oriented and defensive and not oriented to the efforts of the students as earlier publicity had been. Clearly the days of Edna Ferber "reading in the morning," and Allen Ginsberg "reading in the afternoon," days of Vincent Price and Mrs. Udall and other notables abounding on campus, had waned.

There was a new administration in Washington—one that espoused regional control and self-determination. Self-determination in Bureau educational matters worked best for local tribes making determinations about their local schooling but who could or would speak in behalf of so many tribes so far from their home areas? Sensing weaknesses in the Institute structure as it related to Bureau policy, the regional offices began to scrutinize more closely the Institute's entire operation. In keeping with its policies, the Bureau began to lessen its efforts in publicizing the Institute and promoting funding for its programs on the national level. Regional Bureau administration, long irked by what they felt was favoritism showed to the Institute by Washington officials, turned a deaf ear to many of its requests for program funding, staff training, and facilities allocations. Money for an expanded recruitment program had also not been forthcoming.

Indeed, as Rainer and his group of evaluators had noted in 1970, "the IAIA had reached a critical point in its history." Nevertheless, undaunted and optimistic, New pushed forward with the building of an outdoor theatre in 1969 which had been allocated for in 1965 and designed by Paolo Soleri. He also continued to prepare numerous treatises on education, based on cultural differences and continued his proposals and planning for a four-year college.

The objectives for the Institute's program for the fall of 1971 were stated quite simply as follows:

1) To prepare students to gain professional status in the arts and crafts fields.
2) To prepare students to enter college or pursue advanced studies in specialized schools.
3) To prepare students to become gainfully employed in arts related occupations.

In the early fall of 1972, an evaluation report, conducted by the Regional Education Office, Division of Education and Program Review, in Albuquerque, New Mexico, undertook an extensive evaluation of the Institute's program. From its beginning to the end report, this evaluation took one and one half years and was conducted by John Tippeconnie, assisted by John C. Rainer (then a member of IAIA's Board of Regents), Henry H. Rosenbluth, Administration Specialist of the BIA; Thomas R. Hopkins, Evaluation Specialist of the BIA; Roy Bontista, IAIA high school student; David C. Young, Art Specialist of the BIA; Gene Fulgenzie, Acting Principal, IAIA; Millard Holbrook, Acting Assistant Arts Director, IAIA; and Barbara Cameron, student in the IAIA post-graduate program.

Their report was called a "Transition Evaluation," as it questioned a new direction for the institution.

After a review of the background of the IAIA, a list of fifteen tentative goals was developed by the specialists assigned to the evaluation team. These fifteen goals were translated into a questionnaire that was sent to a sample population of 350. This grouping included college students, high school students, parents, staff, former students, and tribal leaders. The questionnaire results, the information in the background paper, and deliberations by the team, culminated in the conclusion that a plausible goal for the Institute was: "to develop a four-year college with emphasis on the Indian Arts and Cultural Studies."

The team further defined the characteristics of such a college: 1) the four-year college development would have a priority in the funding structure, 2) the nature of arts would be associated with those of the American Indians, 3) the cultural studies aspects of the Institute would be an addition to the general concept of the school and would represent a new dimension, 4) when possible, the four-year college should be manned by Indians, 5) Indian people at the tribal level should be involved in developing their own cultural studies aimed at the preservation of their Indian lifeways (to be fostered by the IAIA), and 6) the curriculum should be Indian-based.

The team noted that although the four-year college concept had considerable support, it was not the only educational path that the IAIa might choose to follow. If it were to be followed, the team noted that it indicated a direction of "high order of scholarship and training in the professions as contrasted with training in the vocations." The team further stated that, "It means professional artists rather than vocationally oriented artists, and of equal importance is the concept of scholarship" and a type of "rigor [of scholarship] that a junior college or general high school does not have."

The transition team came to conclusions very similar to Rainer's group. Both groups felt that the faculty and staff were strong, and each discovered the low ration of students to staff and faculty with the attendant high cost of such ratios. Although the Institute could boast of many services available to the students, the students were unaware of most services available to them. There was no strong student organization, drug and alcohol program, or formalized method of communicating between staff and students for out-of-class activities. Both groups concluded that a stronger bond should exist between the academic and art programs. Both teams stressed the importance of the Congress, the New Mexico Legislature, or a Tribal group endorsing the Institute concept, the formation of an independent governing board, and the immediate seeking of accreditation for the postgraduate program. The Transition Team, however, saw more potential for the high school than did Rainer's group, as they considered it to be the logical "feeder" for the Institute-proposed, four-year college. Both groups acknowledged that the present funding system could sustain a high school and junior college, but not a four-year college.

The two greatest weaknesses that both teams found were lack of campus-wide communication and weakness of general administration. Such a lack of direction, communication, and routine administration was felt to be especially regrettable in view of the still remaining high public image of the IAIA and the loyalty and enthusiasm given to the Institute by its students, staff, and faculty.

Since the end of Boyce's administration, reported the evaluation team, no sustained effort had been made to evaluate the Institute's programs or to evaluate the students' progress other than some standardized testing and grade reports. No attempts were made on a yearly basis to ascertain the effectiveness of the faculty's teaching or to document the end results of their teaching on the lives of former students. Some records on former students were just beginning to be gathered in 1973 as an individual effort on the part of one of the new staff members. Such a lack of evaluation and information was seen to make long-range planning extremely difficult, if not nearly impossible.

The Transition Team endorsed a structure for the IAIA that would retain grades eleven and twelve and develop a four-year college, with the cultural studies component having a lesser function than the arts aspect. The cultural studies emphasis of the program would be more closely linked with the high school, seeking outside funding, and working closely with tribal communities, colleges, and universities. They also recommended long-range planning as a top priority followed next by improving campus communication.

In the fall of 1972, the New Mexico State Department of Education sent in a team of education specialists to re-evaluate for accreditation all apsects of the high school program. Their conclusion, although focused particularly on the high school curriculum and teacher performance, echoed the Rainer and Tippenconnie reports. The State Department of Education evaluators, however, unanimously agreed that the ninth and tenth grades should be reinstated as they felt creativity should be fostered at the earliest possible age. The Fine Arts Specialist, Rollie Heltman, reported the most inadequacies in the program, noting that the music program was much too small and inadequately supplied, the dance classes under-enrolled, and that the drama program was limited and staffed by an underqualified instructor. Heltman asked the question in this report, "Does the four years of experience, grades 11, 12, 13, and 14 provide sufficient time to fulfill the objective of gaining professional status in the arts and crafts, music, dance, and drama?"[3]

This question was foremost in the minds of all the evaluators of the IAIA program from 1970 to 1973. If the Institute saw itself as a budding cultural research center for the study of Native American arts, and if it felt itself no longer committed to the earlier philosophy of developing not a professional artist/student but the whole person through the arts, then could it remain a four-year, lower level program? New, the newly formed Board of Regents, and some of the faculty and staff of the IAIA felt it could not.

Opponents to the concept of four year programming could express a number of doubts about its workability, such as: 1) The Bureau had no mechanism for supporting, funding, or operating a four-year institution. 2) The Civil Service regulations provided for only secondary teachers. 3) Was the Bureau obligated to or in a position to provide cultural training to a multi-cultural grouping? 4) Administration and administrative staff could not be properly supplied out of a Civil Service pool which did not require Ph.D's, CPA's, and other specialized degrees for employment in educational managerial positions. 5) Such a program would be extremely expensive relative to other BIA programs. 6) In an era of tribal self-determination, could such training be best provided by regional tribal groups? 7) Would the regional office of the BIA, dedicated to administering regional programs, provide the kind of assistance and support that would be needed for such a unique undertaking?

8) What would become of the many staff and faculty who had built the Institute but who would no longer be qualified to work there? 9) Would college students accept the boarding school regimen associated with the Bureau? 10) If not, could the students maintain themselves off-campus in the small tourist-oriented city of Santa Fe?

While these ideological battles were being waged, the school continued on in its routine. The Transition Report team sparked a flurry of administrative activity even before its final report was submitted. Under New's direction, and with Commissioner Louis Bruce's approval, an independent Board of Regents was formed for the IAIA in 1972. This board consisted of prominent Indian persons from ten geographical areas, all of whom heartily backed New's concept of a four-year arts/culture center for the Santa Fe campus. This board, recommended by both evaluation teams, came about as a result of a directive of Commissioner Bruce in 1970. In this directive, issued to Area Directors and Superintendents, Bruce supported Indian community involvement through school board planning and eventual control of Indian schools.

New also set in motion staff, faculty, and student efforts toward establishing a stronger student senate, a student handbook, a staff and faculty handbook, an alcohol and drug program, a museum apprenticeship program in cooperation with the Museum of New Mexico, and actively pursued avenues of accreditation for the post-secondary courses with the College of Santa Fe, the Rhode Island School of Design, Antioch, and other four-year institutions. Many of these efforts concerning students, staff, and faculty took several years to effect (the formal accreditation process took until 1975 to get formally underway).

Most immediately promising in the early years of the seventies were a series of materials that began to be developed by the faculty and staff, relating the arts to the teaching of Indian children. A forward looking filmmaking program was developed also during this time, giving the student many new avenues of expression. The museum training program, begun in 1971, had quickly become one of the favored areas of specialization among the students and as a result, high quality shows were shown on a regular basis in the museum on campus and large numbers of travelling exhibits were sent out yearly by the students under the direction of James McGrath, Art Director, and later Charles Dailey, Museum Director. The efforts of the Museum training program brought the most favorable publicity to the IAIA during the years 1971 through 1978.

As a result of the state Department of Education's recommendations, it was decided by the administration to reinstate the ninth and tenth grades for a short time and they did so in the early seventies. However, no lower level students were accepted after 1973-74.

The day-to-day operation of the IAIA became increasingly difficult after the formation of the American Indian Movement (AIM) in 1968. Many of the students became caught up in the militancy of the AIM organization after Russell Means, its leader, visited the IAIA campus. AIM activities in Washington, D.C. and at Wounded Knee in 1973 greatly disrupted the campus routine. New, as Boyce and Mackey before him, had been constantly plagued with student behavioral problems and the effects of alcohol and drugs on the students' performance. Campus disruption brought on by outside militancy added another dimension to an already difficult situation.

In 1972, *Arizona Highways* published a lengthy article on the Institute, co-authored by New and the magazine's editor, Joseph Stacey. The article, based on New's frequently published philosophy statement, *Education Based on Cultural Differences*, and incorporating parts of the publication, *Indian Arts I*, was extremely flattering to New's direction of the IAIA program. Stacey's characterization of the nature of the student body, however, was unsettling and could only draw further critical attention to the Institute's problems and give the dreaded impression that its purpose was to supply the arts as therapy. Stacey says of the students:

> Most of the young people have suffered cultural conflict and economic deprivation. They are beset with misunderstandings regarding race, color and religion: and are lost in a labyrinth, in search of identity: they are stung by memories of discrimination. Among them are the revolutionists, the non-conformists, and the unacademically-minded who find no satisfaction in the common goals set for them in the typical school program. They typify that percentage of creative individuals to be found in all cultural groups who seek new ways of self-expression and who are bent on searching out very personal and creative approaches to problem-solving. Holding standards which are at odds with the majority, they reject and are rejected by the typical school program.
>
> Without the opportunity to attend a school catering to their particular drives, such students are most likely to join ranks with the growing number of dropouts who represent one of today's major problems in education. Such misfits, when measured in terms of their ultimate contributions to humanity, very often stand in indictment of a system which categorically has excluded them.[4]

This sort of description, however accurate and sympathetic, only fueled the fires of BIA regional misunderstanding of the Institute's curricular thrust. In 1974, the Board of Regents reported that the "BIA educational authorities in the Indian Education Resource Center, BIA and the Albuquerque Area office came together and unilaterally decided to subvert the Institute's arts education mission to that of meeting the needs of "problem" students [who had been] previously served in an off-reservation school." The Board of Regents further reports that it took on this battle fighting it through to the Washington office where the Albuquerque directive was finally recinded by Commissioner Morris Thompson.

The Institute administrative staff, taking into consideration factors which would make the fulfilling of a four-year college most difficult in this sort of political climate, decided in 1974 to abandon the four-year college concept for a time and pursue a two-year associate of arts degree, having full accreditation and the sponsorship of the Interior Department. The Board of Regents, still dedicated to the four-year cultural institute concept, nonetheless threw itself into a difficult battle of warding off the regional directive along with seeking the sponsorship needed to validate the Institute's program and make it eligible for application for accreditation.

This struggle, as Charles Poitras, Vice President of the IAIA in 1974, said, "was typical of the Institute's constant battle to define its philosophy and validate its mission."

During the early years of the seventies, in an additional effort to gain recognition, the Boards of Regents of the three national Indian post-secondary schools, IAIA, Haskell Institute in Lawrence, Kansas and Southwestern Indian Polytechnic Institute (SIPI) in Albuquerque, joined together in an Associated Board of Regents. "The purpose of this association," said the Regents, "was to form a more workable modus operandi for their respective schools and to strengthen the consortium of the three institutions." Such a consortium had been recommended by the Bureau in the evaluations it had conducted at each institution from 1970 to 1973. The most serious problem these boards faced, as their report states, was "the concern of the area offices for their own local interests which placed the post-secondary institutions in a low priority position for badly needed services and assistance."

Institute personnel, still optimistic, published a recommended degree program in their 1973 and 1974 catalogs to assist the students to plan their two year program so it could easily mesh with the "pending . . . establishment of IAIA as a fully accredited four-year college."

In April of 1975, commissioner of Indian Affairs Morris Thompson issued to the Acting Director of the Albuquerque Area Office, a charter, authorized by the Interior Department, for the operation of at the IAIA of a two-year junior college and separate eleventh and twelfth grade high school program. This was the official recognition that the Institute had needed to begin seeking accreditation. This charter enabled the IAIA to offer to all Indians, Eskimos, and Aleuts of the U.S. of one-fourth Indian blood, an Associate of Fine Arts degree.

The articles of the charter stated that a student might attend one or the other of the programs, and need not attend the high school to be admitted to the junior college. It also authorized the offering of continuing education classes in existing experimental areas of curriculum.

The Albuquerque Area office was instructed to immediately prepare a plan of fiscal operations for the IAIA to be submitted to Thompson. The curricular and fiscal control of the IAIA was put under the charge of the Institute's Board of Regents, who were also officially recognized by the Department of Interior through this Act. In establishing a method of evaluation for the junior college concept, Thompson stated, "The main evaluation criteria for judging the results of such an educational system shall be those that measure how well the system produces graduates who contribute not only to the viability of the general society but to the American Indian community from which they come."

The staff of the Institute was greatly encouraged by this move on Thompson's part. Recognition by the Bureau gave IAIA the formal sanction they had never had. Thompson's support of the Board of Regents and explicit instructions to the Regional office to attend to the Institute's funding, gave the IAIA the most solid official recognition it had received in almost a decade.

Charles Poitras voiced his optimism saying, "We are talking about the creation of a major, national Indian culture center as well as a college . . . The staff of the Institute is working hard to develop an educational program that will help us be what we should be and do what we should do within five years." He also noted that approval of the charter put tremendous responsibility on the IAIA faculty to plan campus expansion, student recruitment, fund raising activities, curriculum development, staffing patterns, and program coordination. Poitras hypothesized that in time the Institute would be a cultural institution, unique in concept, having an "interrelated curriculum in the arts and in Indian culture." He envisioned a center for symposium workshops involving the Indian community and the Santa Fe community with a broad range of programs in drama, dance, architecture, cinematography, and environmental studies along with non-degree courses. "We are talking about the creation of a major national cultural center," he concluded.

The IAIA administration set about immediately to seek and plan for accreditation for the A.F.A. and high school programs from the North Central Accrediting Association. For the upper school, they sought accreditation from the National Association of Schools of Arts, as well.

The year 1975 was an extremely important year to all Indian groups, as it was the year that Congress passed the Indian Self-Determination and Educational Assistance Act (Public Law 93-638, enacted January 4, 1975). This Act was the most significant piece of legislation relating to Indian welfare since 1934 and the Indian Reorganization Act. It noted the federal government's intention to transfer many federally directed programs and services to the control of the Indians. The term *Indian* was defined to mean a tribal governing body or its representative. Financing, a matter of primary concern, would be underwritten by the federal government through contracts and grants. Thompson devoted the next two years to advancing among the tribes the ways and means for using this Act for their purposes.

The passage by Congress of the Self-Determination Act, signalled the choices tribes would begin to exercise for providing the kinds of schooling they wished for their youth, and would greatly affect the Institute's future direction and enrollment.

Since 1964 when New published *Education for Cultural Differences*, he had gone on record as being dedicated to culture-based education. In this sense, he and the staff at IAIA that supported his efforts were very much in the forefront of supporting education for ethnic groups and had provided the impetus for other Indian schools to revise their curricular and educational philosophies, based on IAIA concepts. The Black movement, which saw its greatest strength in the sixties and early seventies, caused colleges and universities across the country to establish Black Studies programs. Many public schools responded by revising textbooks at all levels to include the Black experience and they developed courses to foster for all their students an appreciation of Black culture. In much the same way, after the formation of AIM and other Native American groups in the late sixties and early seventies, Native American Studies programs were established at many colleges and universities. Some schools, using Title IV or Johnson O'Malley funding, responded by enlarging their library collections of Indian-related materials or establishing courses on Native American history and literature. These efforts were small, however, compared to the efforts extended to the Black minority.

By 1974, Bureau schools, in general lagging a decade behind public schools, revised their educational goals. A number of these goals, depicted below, aimed at Bureau schools serving grades one through fourteen, related to the cultural aspects of academic and vocatonal training.

Under goals for citizenship training:

Students should demonstrate the attainment of; and understanding and respect for different cultures as well as the learner's own heritage and culture.

An awareness of the contribution of many different peoples and the interdependence and interrelationship among peoples, regions, and nations.

Under goals for the Humanities and arts:

Students should acquire a background in one or more of the arts which will provide an understanding of the interrelationship of the arts and humanizing influence of man's struggle to recreate his inner self in some observable art form, and in verbal language.

Students should have an understanding and appreciation of the cultural contributions which the arts of their own people and others have made to literature, art, music, and folklore of the nation.

The Bureau's obligation to Diverse Cultural Groups:

All schools should provide a positive learning environment for each student no matter what his cultural and linguistic background may be. Special programs are required to meet the needs of students who are bilingual and/or bicultural.[5]

A wide diversity of programming was now available to Indian youths. They might attend a day school on the reservation, or a public school grades one through eight, later a Bureau high school or a public school near a reservation, or they might choose to attend off-reservation specialty schools such as Haskell, SIPI, or the IAIA. In addition to these opportunities in grades one through fourteen, the students, on equal footing with all American students, could attend the junior college, college, university, or specialty school of their choice. A wide variety of funding was available to students seeking higher education opportunities: Basic Education

Opportunity Grants, Supplemental Education Opportunity Grants, Bureau scholarships, or tribal funding from his/her own tribe. Some funding available to students could be used for study outside the United States. Grants, scholarships, and gifts to Indian students were plentiful and easy to obtain.

As Indian students were increasingly attending public high schools, they received the same career counseling as the other students. It was here that the Institute mechanism suffered its greatest weakness. In areas of recruiting, the IAIA remained consistently underfinanced, and could not compete nationwide with other institutions. The Institute's most effective tool of recruitment had always been word of mouth. Those Indian youths who were urban or without tribal ties, had no relatives who had attended the IAIA, or who feared the restrictions of boarding school life, were not attracted to its program. Others, knowing about the IAIA, but preferring to pursue their art in a four-year institution from the start of their education, chose an integrated existence from the beginning. In addition to these factors, tribes such as the Navajo, the Hopi, and the Sioux had established their own educational programs in higher education, either independently or in conjunction with a nearby state or private college, thereby keeping their young people in training near their home reservations.

The Self-Determination Act so eagerly awaited by all Indian tribes, did not work to the Institute's benefit, but rather tended to draw away students and funds into programs built often times on the Institute model. In the areas of materials development, the educators gathered around the Navajo Community College quickly out-stripped the IAIA staff who were taken up with the concept of an arts junior college, serving a multiplicity of tribes.

The Sioux in South Dakota and the Hopis in Arizona were quick to draw the local tribes into curriculum and materials planning and integrated activities with other educational institutions. The evaluators of the IAIA in the early seventies had all recommended cultural education materials development and training for teachers of Indian children as the Institute's most important potential contributions to Indian education. Indeed, Institute personnel repeatedly stated that one of its foremost goals was to become a major cultural resource center and the evaluation teams saw this stated function as being most effective when carried out with the many tribes the IAIA served.

The 1975-76 catalog of the IAIA states that:

The IAIA is presently moving toward the formation of a major

115

cultural institution that can assume responsibility for serving the entire Indian community and the nation as a focal point for recognition of Indian culture.

Such a bold and optimistic statement, in view of prevailing national and tribal thought, continued to be a good indicator of the level of idealism, energy, and pride with which New and his staff attacked each redefinition of their "mission."

Faced with further budget cuts, and cuts in programming which had all but eliminated dance, drama, filmmaking, and music, the staff in 1975 revised the IAIA curricular goals and objectives, remaining fairly consistent with their original purposes but stressing the Institute's primary function as being the delivery of the A.F.A. program and its secondary function as being the development of the cultural approach to education. Plans were laid for activities to develop stronger tribal ties to the Institute and to provide non-degree courses for on and off-campus students. An honors program was also established in this year.

Hank Gobin, alumnus of the IAIA and its Art Director, stated simply the five goals of the upper school program:

1) To prepare students to gain professional status in the arts and crafts fields

2) To prepare students to pursue advanced studies

3) To prepare students to become gainfully employed in arts-related occupations

4) To work with the students' natural talents and cultural strengths

5) . . . And to offer a curriculum equal in scope and quality to that of other nationally recognized accredited schools of a total professional nature.

Fiscal matters were the key to the Institute's future and its hopes for future funding were raised when in August of 1976 the Director of the Office of Indian Education of the BIA ordered the transfer of Haskell, SIPI, and the IAIA from regional control to a central office control in Washington, D.C. This mandate was brought about by considerable lobbying by the three Boards of Regents so that their respective institutions might operate more autonomously in fiscal and curricular matters. The three institutions were to jointly develop all fiscal operations. Each was given Linolex computers with which to communicate directly with the Washington office where a supervisory office for the three schools was to be set up and a higher education director was to be hired to work with the three schools. Due to the organization problems of a new administration in the central office, the Regents reported in

1978 that no funds had been provided to train staff to operate the computers, no director of higher education had been appointed, and they (the Regents) were caught in the hopeless situation of answering to the regional and central offices with no guidelines as to which office controlled which aspect of the budget and curricular affairs.

This tug-of-war for funds, when enrollments were steadily declining, was extremely detrimental to staff morale and continuity of programs. The enrollment for the total program at the IAIA in 1976 was 205, with the annual cost per student of $10,453. The annual cost per student had risen steadily at the IAIA as the high school grades were discontinued and the postgraduate enrollments had proportionally decreased. An additional factor in ascribing these costs was the high rate of student attrition due to programatic cutbacks in dance, music, drama, and so on. SIPI, a vocational/technical training school, listed its cost per student for the same year at approximately $1,000 less, and Haskell, a two-year liberal arts/vocational school, at one half the cost. A vicious cycle had set in firmly at the Institute — cutbacks in programs meant fewer students, fewer students meant less fiscal allocations, less funding meant more cutbacks. Once this cycle had begun it could only be reversed by an unexpectedly large enrollment or an unexpectedly large budget. Neither of these were forthcoming and the fiscal struggle for survival went on in deadly earnest.

Hampered by all of the factors pertaining to its declining enrollment, the Institute personnel prepared for the arrival of the accrediting teams from North Central and the National Association of Schools of Art in 1977. Publicity, which had been allowed to flag, was sought for museum shows and other student activities, an effort was made to put together continuing education courses (open to Indians only), and plans were put in motion for summer teacher workshops and campus cultural activities open to the public.

In 1977 as well, a formal liaison effort was begun with the College of Santa Fe. The College of Santa Fe, a Christian Brothers institution, had served IAIA post-secondary students since 1962, but although there had been various fits and starts at program integration and exchange, these efforts had not been formalized. In the summer of 1977 this writer, then the Director of the Visual Arts Program at the College of Santa Fe (Visual Arts major established in 1974), petitioned and received a three-year grant through federal Title III Higher Education funding to employ a full-time person versed in Indian education to work with the art program at the College of Santa Fe and the IAIA, to bring the two organizations together in an exchange of students, facilities, and events.

This venture assisted Institute students in finding a near-by fully-accredited institution where they might apply their two-year AFA degrees, or courses at the Institute, toward a four-year degree in visual arts. Such an arrangement was desperately needed as accreditation for the Institute's program, with its vagaries of Civil Service appointments, cancelled programs, underqualified staff, and lack of fiscal ability to expand, would be greatly delayed for the Institute.

The Self-Determination Act had also unlocked an old question: should the Santa Fe BIA campus serve its regional tribes? Was the Institute, with its declining enrollment and two-year art program, really serving the needs of the students from the eighty tribes that it served, or could those students be better served close to their home reservations? Could the Santa Fe campus in the center of the Pueblo communities better serve the Pueblo Indians? Could the Institute arts students be better served in four-year colleges and universities? All were valid and pressing questions in view of current legislation. By 1978, the old SFIS-IAIA battle was revived among some of the Pueblo tribes and took on new strength as the Institute program weakened.

In 1977 the IAIA's Board of Regents, attempting to seek a solution to the curricular focus and mission of the Institute, organized a two-day conference to be held at the College of Santa Fe. Fifty-three noted Indian writers, visual artists, playwrights, filmmakers, dancers, and composers, plus some Institute personnel and Bureau persons, along with non-Indian persons (this writer was included as an observer but allowed to participate fully), to seek a solution to the Institute's problems and set a direction or focus for its program. In October, 1978, a report assembled by Dr. Helen Red-Bird Selam, President of the Board of Regents, was distributed to all who participated and to Institute and Bureau personnel. Of the major recommendations relating to every aspect of the IAIA program which were put forward, Recommendation V sums up the findings of the group when it stated that the IAIA must be freed from its "bureaucratic restraints." The report states that, "There seemed to be the consensus that it is questionable whether the Bureau of Indian Affairs can really develop a major cultural institution of Indian people with its past history of assimilation practices and its present hiring policies that are rooted in a Civil Service System." "These processes," concluded the report, "are more fitted to the armed service and less fitted to the development of an outstanding facility of the arts. Ways of developing the institution through some of the new legislation regarding Indian preference and Indian determinism should be explored."

Lloyd New, in reporting on fiscal matters in 1977, said that he had been "so preoccupied with the struggle for survival . . . that other matters, even though serious and pressing, [had] received less than adequate attention." The students too had been caught up in this battle of institutional survival, in some instances the struggle had taken precedence over their own work. Those that did not get actively involved in the fight felt nonetheless the effects of institutional uncertainty through the low morale and discontent of some of the faculty and staff.

The creative output of the school fell into decline and repetition. The visual arts became, with some exceptions, second-generation-eclectic, drawing on the work of faculty and students of the sixties. What was considered by some to be a "New School of Indian Art," was as subject to repetition and cliche as had been the a "traditional" work of the SFIS. Younger students, hoping to emulate the work of former students in the Santa Fe area who were now finding considerable financial success, looked to their works rather than to a broad spectrum of world arts and cultural traditions as had the students of the sixties.

The large number of IAIA alumni on the arts teaching staff was partly responsible for this inbreeding of artistic style and subject matter. The Indian Preference Act, as interpreted in the seventies by the Civil Service System, greatly inhibited the hiring of highly-trained professionals of various backgrounds and reputations in the arts. The intention of the reaffirmation of this Act in 1972 was to encourage the upward mobility of Indian employees. In the case of the IAIA it all but made impossible the hiring of a non-Indian faculty member if an Indian had applied for the position. Understandably, Institute alumni were anxious to rejoin the excitement they had known there as students, but some came back to the Institute well-trained while others did not. Unfortunately the very excitement they remembered and sought had been futher inhibited by such inbreeding and closeness to their student days. The highly eclectic vitality of the arts of the sixties at the IAIA gave way in the middle seventies to a complacent redundancy. Such a yearning for the "glorious past" greatly stifled creative growth among the students and faculty as well.

Alvin M. Josephy, Jr., upon evaluation the Institute's program in 1976, writes: "The Institute is a distinctly unique and important national institution. However, the U.S. Government, which administers the school, has failed to show interest in this fact. Specifically . . . with only minor and tentative exceptions . . . the BIA, the BIA's parent body, the Department of Interior; the Indian section of the Office of Management and Budget; the Interior liaison people at the White House; and the staffs and membership of the Senate and House Committees on Interior and Insular Affairs, have all failed to recognize both the achievements and potential of the Institute and have been guilty of wasting taxpayers' funds by permitting the creation of a school of which the whole nation should be, and can be, proud, and then letting it struggle along in a helpless, underfunded condition, saddling it with senseless bureaucratic difficulties, and giving it neither the attention nor support it requires and merits."[6]

In the spring of 1978, Lloyd New announced his retirement from the Bureau. A few months later the IAIA graduated its last high school class and its first A.F.A. group. It had been a long hard fight for New, with some battles won, and many others of utmost importance to him, lost. A four-year arts institution and a national culture center did not seem forthcoming for the Institute. A wide variety of arts offerings were now outside the financial grasp of the institution. The image of the IAIA had faded, commanding little national or international attention and the support of influential persons as it had in the past. It has struggled so hard for survival and recognition since it chose to alter its original purpose, that its students, faculty, and staff were worn out from the fight.

To honor Lloyd New in his departure, the museum training students hung a show of works done by faculty and prominent alumni from the years 1962-1978 entitled, *Rings of Growth*. In his last public interview in the *New Mexican*, New predicted "better days" saying:

> Despite BIA intentions to help Indians, the too frequent result of BIA attention has been "cultural genocide."
>
> We're a stubborn race who doesn't get much satisfaction from being a part of the American scene. A few years ago, with the rise of the civil rights movement, there was a world-wide recognition of cultural pluralism and the fact that people could live side by side without the stronger eating up the weaker.
>
> The BIA recognizes this now, but they can't get under it. It's as if they don't really know how to. It's much easier for them to do the other thing, to support the old idea that the sooner Indians stop being Indians and start being white people, the better off they'll be. The

government just doesn't seem to know how to make amends. There was very little opportunity until the last decade for Indians to have any input into the system, whatever it was. But Federal policy now says Indians should hold positions that influence policy.

But Indians doing that need to be able to analyze what's happening. And they can do that through effective education which emphasizes the cultural aspect . . . we need thinking Indians in those positions.

. . . I see a real battle shaping up [around the IAIA] in the next six months and I don't intend to just sit on the sidelines.

At an Indian dance or meeting, things move in a straight line. People gather and wait, and sometimes nothing happens. Other times, all the energy comes together, and things move in a wave-like manner towards a high point. But there is no beginning or end to an Indian ceremony . . . nor is there any end to the potential for the IAIA.

Insitutue of American Indian Arts Museum

AFTERWORD

"There is no beginning or end to an Indian ceremony—nor is there any
end to the potential for the IAIA. . . ."   Lloyd New

These words spoken by Lloyd New upon his retirement from
the Institute in 1978 ring especially true in this the twenty-fifth year
of the IAIA's continuous existence. The IAIA has undergone a great
many changes in the intervening years since New's departure, but it
appears to be closer at this time to becoming what New had envisioned it should become, than ever before. To reach this crucial
point in its history a great many changes were forced on this strug-
gling institution and many supportive persons came forward to de-
fend it and build for its future.

The two most significant events in the Institute's recent history
were the appointment of Jon Wade (Flauderaeau Sioux) in 1979 as
president and the physical move of the school to a new location in
1981. One cannot disucss one event without the other.

Wade, like George Boyce of the sixties' era, had a flair for dealing with the bureaucracy and had come to the Institute with an extensive background in BIA education. Jon Wade, an energetic,
pragmatic, and determined, administrator was an excellent choice
for the Institute as it was entering a new phase of its development.
Wade, rather than being put off by bureaucratic red tape, took such
difficulties as challenges to be overcome and handily dealt with. He
was ably assisted by Dave Warren (Santa Clara), Director of the Institute's Cultural Studies Resource and Research Center, who had
carried the additional burden of acting-president before Wade's arrival. Together they made a most effective team: Wade the seasoned
Bureau educator/administrator and Warren, known throughout the
national and international arts community for his pursuance of
cultural and ethnic education methodology.

Wade and Warren, along with the IAIA staff, tackled the for-
midable problems facing the IAIA in the late seventies and early
eighties: a severe decline in enrollment, dramatic cutting back of
staff, budget cuts, and curtailment of academic and arts programs.
These problems were further compounded by the pressure being
put on the BIA by the All-Indian Pueblo Council (AIPC) to turn the
IAIA campus over to the Council for use as a junior and senior high
school for area Pueblo children.

After much debate, the BIA and IAIA agreed in 1979 that
students from the Albuquerque Indian School should be transferred

to the Institute campus for training in the tenth, eleventh, and twelfth grades supervised by the Pueblo Council. This was to be a temporary arrangement until the Albuquerque campus could be renovated. However, the sentiment that had been building over the years amongst the Pueblo peoples that the IAIA campus was the location where they wished to have their children schooled, grew dramatically with this move. Delfin Lavato, Chairman of the Pueblo Council, gained the support of the Secretary of the Interior, James Watt, and Senator Pete Domenici of New Mexico. Together they worked on legislation that gave the Pueblos control of the entire IAIA campus for use as a junior and senior high school. Used as rationale for this legislation by the AIPC were the assumptions that the Institute was under-using the Santa Fe campus and that it was unlikely that federal renovation funds would be forthcoming to make the Albuquerque campus safe and liveable for the students. At one point in the debate Lavato proposed taking over the operation of the Institute as well, but this proposal did not find adequate support in Congress.

The administration of the IAIA was abruptly given three choices by the Bureau, short of the closing the school: move the Institute to the old Albuquerque Indian School campus, move it to Haskell Institute in Kansas, or somehow find suitable quarters for the IAIA in Santa Fe. Faced with this dilemma Jon Wade felt he had no choice. He felt that to stay on and continue to fight the Pueblo Council over the use of his present campus would in the long run prove fruitless and divisive. However, he also strongly felt that the IAIA needed to stay in Santa Fe where fifty years of contact with the Indian and non-Indian art cultures of the Southwest had helped to build the school's and the area's identity as the center for Indian arts. Without this identity and this outlet for the students' production, the school's future would be seriously damaged. Against the wishes of many of his staff and students, Wade approached the College of Santa Fe (CSF) seeking a temporary home for the Insitute.

As good fortune would have it, the IAIA and the College of Santa Fe had long ago established a sound working relationship. They had put into operation in the years 1976-81 an experimental exchange program of students and teachers and some shared facilties. In addition, many Institute students continued to come to the CSF to complete a four year degree. The College was also at this time experiencing budget difficulties based on declining enrollment. It appeared immediately that a physical merging of the two schools would come as a boon to both institutions. In the spring of 1981 an agreement was worked out by the authorities of the CSF and the IAIA to lease to the IAIA quarters on the CSF campus for classes, athletic activities, dormitory space, space for portable classrooms, and cafeteria services. The IAIA also worked out an agreement with the BIA and the Pueblo Council to maintain its museum and three-dimensional course studios at what had now become "The SFIS" campus.

The Institute opened its classes in the fall of 1981 at the CSF, and continues its lease agreement with the College at this time. The students of both accredited colleges may take courses from either institution and many Institute A.F.A. graduates stay on to finish a four-year degree at the College. Although IAIA students continue to fear their loss of institutional identity and hope for their own campus, they also comment that they have benefitted from being a day-to-day part of a four year institution.

After its move to the CSF the IAIA continued to be severely criticized by government authorities for its low enrollment. The cost of educating a student at the IAIA was and continued to be much higher than that of other BIA junior colleges. Wade, and his staff, had made this problem their focus while still on their "old" campus. Declining enrollment had continued to translate into cuts in staffing and programs. These cuts in turn meant less interest was manifested by potential students. Wade and his staff again attacked this problem with vigor. Today the Institute's enrollment is higher than it has been since the late seventies, numbering more than 180 full-time students.

Throughout the move and other difficulties Wade, the IAIA staff, students, supporters, and the Institute Board of Regents, pushed for state and national legislation that would provide funding for a new campus and museum for the Institute. Along with these thrusts they also worked with the BIA and Congress to provide the means of releasing the Institute from some of the restrictive bonds imposed by the BIA and allow it to become more of an independent art school and cultural center. Such an arrangement would provide for independent fund raising, private and foundation support and the eventual release of the Institute's staff from the constraints of federal civil service regulations. Those working toward this legislation argued that if these requests were granted, in time the IAIA could manage to establish its own campus and increase its course offerings to a four-year program and beyond. In essence, these proposals were very much like those Lloyd New had made many years before.

It would seem that such a difficult mission could break the morale and bend the determination of such a small institution. This has been far from the case. The media, the public, and state and national legislators began to take note of the courage and devotion of these immensely dedicated people. The IAIA alumni, now gaining in age and influence, rallied to its support and a new enthusiasms began to flow through its temporary quarters, reduced staff, and beleaguered students.

In 1986 all these efforts came to fruition when Congress passed the *American Indian, Alaska Native, and Native Hawaiian Culture and Development Act.* By this act the status of the Institute has been changed from a directly funded BIA entity to a chartered institution much like the Smithsonian. This act will enable the Institute to receive government funding, yet have its own governing board, solicit private funding, phase out its civil service personnel system for the one of its own making, and in other ways to act as a nonprofit corporation. The national governing board designated by the act is currently being selected and must be approved by the President of the United States.

Needless to say, all who have supported and worked so hard to promote the ideals of the Insitute over the years are delighted at the passage of this act. They do not feel, however, that the struggle is over. A great deal of hard work will have to go into developing this new institution under new federal guidelines. But if the past can be used as a forecaster of the determination of those supporting the Institute concept then they stand a very good chance of succeeding.

Perhaps, the most encouraging news of all surrounding the IAIA is that in the past few years the arts at the Institute, like the institution itself, have become revitalized. The stale imitations of the sixties' arts, accepted by many of the students of the seventies, are no longer tolerated by the majority of the students of the eighties. New images are being sought, new media, new opportunites for showing, and new ways to develop arts careers after the IAIA experience, are flourishing. A new community of creative, innovative, and searching IAIA alumni has begun to build up in the Santa Fe area. Friendships amongst these artists are strong and the exchange of ideas frequent. It is significant that in the midst of tremendous institutional struggle the students of this unique institution once again came together in a diversity of ways and for a diversity of reasons to find a new artistic focus for their chosen school. If one is the judge the worth of the Institute or look for indicators of its success or failure one cannot ignore the most important contributions, those made by the students themselves. There can be no doubt based on student performance and enthusiasm that the Institute deserves a long life.

Neither can there be any doubt, when one visits the museums and galleries of the Southwest and major cities of this country and abroad, of the influence of the IAIA students past and present, on the arts public and on non-Indian artists. This tradition which began so quietly so many years ago when SFIS Supt. DeHuff encouraged Indian students to draw and paint in his home has grown into what is now on the eve of becoming the newly formed, *Institute of American Indian and Alaska Native Culture and Arts Development.*

Jon Wade, like other Institute directors and presidents before him, has been reassigned and now works in South Dakota. Most of the other staff members who assisted him in his fight to gain independence for the Institute have stayed on to work toward the Institute's new status. The Institute Museum, under Chuck Dailey's direction, continues to thrive at its old location sending out shows selected from its 4,000 art works across the nation and countries abroad.

These are good and promising times for the Institute of American Indian Arts. Its future as a center of Native American art seems to be finally assured.

I
NOTES

1 Kvasnicka, Robert M. and Herman J. Viola, *The Commissioner of Indian Affairs, 1824-1977* (Lincoln: University of Nebraska Press, 1979), p. 199.

2 Edward Everett Dale, *The Indians of the Southwest* (Norman: University of Oklahoma Press, 1976), p. 75.

3 Estelle Fuchs and Robert J. Havinghurst, *To Live on This Earth*, p. 5.

4 Dale, p. 176.

5 Dale, p. 176.

6 Dale, p. 176.

7 Dale, p. 177.

8 Frances Paul Prucha, *Education Documents of United States Indian Policy* (Lincoln: University of Nebraska Press, 1975), p. 201.

9 Prucha, p. 174.

10 Howard E. Fay and D'Arcy McNickel, *Indians and Other Americans* (New York: Harper and Row, 1970), p. 82.

11 Prucha, p. 200.

12 Fuchs and Havinghurst, p. 6.

13 Horatio Oliver Ladd, "Founding of Santa Fe Indian Industrial School," *Santa Fe New Mexican*, 25 September 1925, p. 1.

14 "Santa Fe Indian School," *Santa Fe Weekly New Mexican*, 28 June 1885, p. 4.

15 Dale, p. 178.

16 Dale, p. 184.

17 "Santa Fe United States Industrial School," *Ranch and Range*, February 1901, p. 14.

18 Billy Joe Bryant, "Issues of Art Education for American Indians in the Indian Affairs School," Diss. Pennsylvania State University, 1974, pp. 61-62.

19 Bryant, p. 63.

20 Prucha, pp. 178-180.

21 E.L. Hewett, *Ancient Life in the American Southwest* (Indianapolis: Bobbs-Merrell Company, 1930), p. 146.

22 Ernest Carroll Moore, *Fifty Years of American Fiction* (Boston: Ginn and Company, 1917), p. 56.

23 Personal interview with Carmelita Dunlap, 20 November 1974.

24 David Wallace Adams, "The Federal Indian Boarding School: A Study of Environment and Response, 1879-1918," Diss. Indiana University, 1975, pp. 12-15.

25 Harold E. Driver, *Indians of North America* (Chicago: University of Chicago Press, 1961), p. 435.

26 Elsie Clew Parson, *The Social Organization of the Tewa in New Mexico*, No. 38 (1929); rpt. New York: Kraus Reprint Corporation, 1964), p. 5.

27 Louise Udall, *Me and Mine: The Life Story of Helen Sekaquaptewa* (Tucson: University of Arizona Press, 1969), pp. 68-70.
28 Leo W. Simmons, ed., *Sun Chief: An Autobiography of a Hopi Indian*, (New Haven: Yale University Press, 1962), p. 93.
29 Simmons, p. 89.
30 Udall, p. 64.
31 Udall, pp. 19-20.
32 Francis La Flesche, *The Middle Five* (Madison: University of Wisconsin Press, 1963), pp. xvi-xx.
33 La Flesche, pp. xvi-xx.
34 Driver, p. 386.
35 Simmons, pp. 51-52.
36 Simmons, p. 68.
37 Simmons, p. 117.
38 Paul Horgan, *The Centuries of Santa Fe* (New York: E.P. Dutton and Company, 1956), p. 323.
39 Horgan, p. 315.
40 Fuchs and Havinghurst, pp. 9-10.
41 Edna Fergusson, *New Mexico: A Pageant of Three Peoples* (New York: Alfred A. Knopf, 1951), p. 372.
43 Fergusson, p. 372.
44 Austin, p. 266.
45 Austin, p. 361.
46 J.J. Brody, *Indian Painters and White Patrons* (Albuquerque: University of New Mexico Press, 1971), p. 82.
47 Horgan, p. 320.
48 "How Should We Educate the Indian?" *El Palacio*, 11 July 1922, p. 61.
49 Alice C. Henderson, "A Plea for the Study of Indian Culture," *El Palacio*, 6 (15 September 1923), n. pag.
50 "True West Salutes Chester E. Faris," *True West*, 7 (Jan/Feb. 1960), 64.
51 Brody, p. 102.
52 H.G. Hagerman, "The Indians of the Southwest," Memorandum for the Secretary of the Interior and Commissioner of Indian Affairs, Santa Fe, New Mexico, re. "The Indians of the Southwest," mimeographed, 1 July 1931, p. 31.

II

1 Margaret McKittrick, "Lost: A Tradition," *The School Arts Magazine*, 30, No. 7 (1931), 450.
2 Henry J. Albrecht, "Vocational Guidance in the Academic Classroom," *Indian School Journal of Chilocco Indian Industrial School*, January 1932, p. 14.

3   Edwin Lewis Wade, "The History of the Southwest Indian Ethnic Market," Diss. University of Washington, 1976, pp. 50-52.

4   "Indian Art Students: University of New Mexico Plans Unique Experiment to Stimulate Native Talent in New Fields," *El Palacio*, 29, No. 11 (23 September 1930), 182-183.

5   Dorothy Dunn, "Going to School with the Little Domingos," The School Arts Magazine, 30, no. 7 (1931) pp. 473-474.

6   Dorothy Dunn Kramer, "The Studio: 1932-1937—Fostering Indian Art as Art" *El Palacio*, 83, no. 4 (Winter 1977) p. 6.

7   J.J. Brody, *Indian Painters and White Patrons* (Albuquerque: University of New Mexico Press, 1971), p. 55.

8   Houser interview.

9   "Seymour President of Santa Fe and Albuquerque Schools," *Santa Fe New Mexican*, 29 September 1936, p. 2.

10   Velarde interview.

11   Personal interview with Carmelita Dunlap, 20 November 1974.

III

1   Hildegard Thompson, Letter to Dr. George a. Boyce, July 1972, Boyce Papers, held by Mrs. Oleta Boyce, Santa Fe, NM; hereafter cited as Boyce Papers.

2   Dr. George A. Boyce, Letter to Lynn Waugh, 23 July 1972, Boyce Papers.

3   Personal interview with Mrs. Oleta Boyce, 15 May 1977.

4   Mamie L. Mizen, *Federal Facilities for Indians*, U.S. Cong., Senate, Committee on Appropriations (November 1964); rpt. Washington, D.C.: GOP, 1965), pp. 3-10.

5   "Recent Exhibitions — Young American Indian Artists," *Arts Magazine*, February 1966, pp. 52-54.

IV

1   Vina Windes, "World Could Profit from Indians' Values," *The New Mexican*, 13 August 1967, Sec. D, p. 2, cols. 1-6.

2   Robert M. Coates, "Our Far-Flung Correspondents/Indian Affairs, New Style," *The New Yorker*, 17 June 1967, pp. 102, 104-106, 108-112.

3   State of NM, Department of Education, Accreditation Team, *The IAIA Program Review*, "Review of Fine Arts Area," by Rollie Heltman (Santa Fe: n.p., 1972), p. 2.

4   Joseph Stacey, "Institute of American Indian Arts," *Arizona Highways*, January 1972, pp. 13-14.

5   Morris Thompson, Memorandum to all Area Directors, re. "Goals for Indian Education," 7 March 1974, pp. 1-4, Boyce Papers.

6   Alvin M. Josephy, Jr., *National Humanities Faculty Report and visit to the Institute of American Indian Arts, September, 20-21, 1976* (New York: American Heritage Publishing Co., Inc., October —, 1976), p. 1.

LIST OF REFERENCES
BOOKS

Anderson, George B. *History of New Mexico: Its Resources and Its People*. Los Angeles: Pacific States Publishing Co., 1907. Vol. I.

Anderson, Richard L. *Art in Primitive Societies*. Englewood Cliffs, New Jersey: Prentice-Hall, Inc., 1979.

Austin, Mary. *Earth Horizons*. New York: Houghton-Mifflin Co., 1932.

Brody, J.J. *Indian Painters and White Patrons*. Albuquerque: University of New Mexico Press, 1971.

Dale, Edward Everett. *The Indians of the Southwest*. Norman: University of Oklahoma Press, 1976.

Davis, Ellis Arthur, ed. *The Historical Encyclopedia of New Mexico*. Albuquerque: New Mexico Historical Assn., 1945.

Driver, Harold E. *Indians of North America*. Chicago: University of Chicago Press, 1961.

Dunn, Dorothy. *American Indian Painting of the Southwest and Plains Areas*. Albuquerque: University of New Mexico Press, 1968.

Fay, Howard E. and D'Arcy McNickel. *Indians and Other Americans*. New York: Harper and Row, 1970.

Fergusson, Erna. *New Mexico: A Pageant of Three Peoples*. New York: Alfred A. Knopf, 1951.

Fuchs, Estelle and Robert J. Havinghurst. *To Live On This Earth*. Garden City, New York: Anchor Press/Double-Day, 1973.

Good, H. G. *A History of American Education*. New York: The Macmillan Co., 1956.

Grayburn, Nelson H. H., ed. *Ethnic and Tourist Arts, Cultural Expressions from the Fourth World*. Berkeley: University of California Press, 1976.

Hewett, E. L. *Ancient Life in the American Southwest*. Indianapolis: Bobbs-Merrill Co., 1930.

Horgan, Paul. *The Centuries of Santa Fe*. New York: E. P. Dutton and Co., 1956

Josephy, Alvin M., Jr. *National Humanities Facility Report and Visit to the Institute of American Indian Arts, September 20-21, 1976*. New York: American Heritage Publishing Co., Inc., 1976.

Kvasnicka, Robert M. and Herman J. Viola. *The Commissioners of Indian Affairs, 1824-1977*. Lincoln: University of Nebraska Press, 1979.

La Flesche, Frances. *The Middle Five*. Madison: University of Wisconsin Press, 1963.

McNickel, D'Arcy. *Indian Man: A Life of Oliver La Farge*. Bloomington: Indiana University Press, 1971.

Meriam, Lewis. *The Problem of Indian Administration*, for the Brookings Institute. Baltimore: Johns Hopkins Press, 1928.

Mitchell, Emerson Blackhorse and T. D. Allen. *Miracle Hill, The Story of a Navajo Boy.* Norman: University of Oklahoma Press, 1967.

Moore, Ernest Carroll. *Fifty Years of American Education.* Boston: Ginn and Co., 1917.

Parsons, Elsie Clew. *General Series in Anthropology, Taos Pueblo,* No. 2. n.d.; rpt. New York: Johnson Reprint Corp., 1970.

———. *The Social Organization of the Tewa in New Mexico,* No. 38. 1929; rpt. New York: Kraus Reprint Corp., 1964.

Prucha, Francis Paul. *Education, Documents of the United States Indian Policy.* Lincoln: University of Nebraska Press, 1975.

Simmons, Leo., ed. *Sun Chief. An Autobiography of an Hopi Indian.* New Haven: Yale University Press, 1962.

Sloan, John and Oliver La Farge. *Introduction to American Indian Arts.* New York: Exposition of Indian Tribal Arts, Inc., 1931.

Szasz, Margaret. *Education and the American Indian.* Albuquerque: University of New Mexico Press, 1974.

Tanner, Clara Lee. *Southwest Indian Painting.* Tucson: University of Arizona Press, 1957.

Udall, Louise. *Me and Mine. The Life Story of Helen Sekaquaptewa.* Tucson: University of Arizona Press, 1969.

DISSERTATIONS

Adams, David Wallace. "The Federal Indian Boarding School: A study of Environment and Response, 1879-1918." Diss. Indiana University 1975.

Bryant, Billy Joe. "Issues of Art Education for American Indians in the Indian Affairs School." Diss. Pennsylvania State University 1974.

Wade, Edwin Lewis. "The History of the Southwest Indian Ethnic Market." Diss. University of Washington 1976.

PERIODICALS

Coates, Robert M., "Our Far-Flung Correspondents/Indian Affairs, New Style," *The New Yorker,* 17 June 1967, pp. 102, 104-106, 108-112.

"De Huff's Report on Indian Fair," *El Palacio,* 2 (15 September 1926), n. pag.

Dunn, Dorothy, "Going to School With the Little Domingos," *The School Arts Magazine,"* 30, No. 7 (1931), pp. 469-474.

Dunn, Dorothy, "Indian Art in the Schools," *Indians at Work,* 15 August 1935, p. 20.

Dunn, Dorothy, "Indian Children Carry Forward Old Traditions," *The School Arts Magazine,* 34, No. 7 (1935), p. 428.

Henderson, Alice C., "A Plea for the Study of Indian Culture," *El Palacio,* 6 (15 September 1923), no. pag.

"How Should We Educate the Indian?" *El Palacio,* 19 (12 May 1928), pp. 61-62.

"Indian Art at County Schools," *El Palacio*, 19)12 May 1928), n. pag.

"Indian Art Students: University of New Mexico Plans Unique Experiment to Stimulate Native Talent in New Fields," *El Palacio*, 29, No. 11 (23 September 1930), pp. 182-183.

Kramer, Dorothy Dunn, "The Studio: 1932-1937—Fostering Indian Art as Art," *El Palacio*, 83, No. 4 (Winter 1977), pp. 5-6, 8-9.

McKittrick, Margaret, "Lost: A Tradition," *The School Arts Magazine*, 30, No. 7 (1931), p. 450.

"Oklahoman, Lloyd Kiva New, Indian Educator," *Muskogee Area Education News*, September 1972, pp. 1, 4.

Progressive Education: A Review of the Newer Tendencies in Education, 9, No. 2 (February 1932), pp. 87-95, 117-130.

Quick, Bob, "Forging Ahead at 100," *New Mexico Magazine*, Vol. 65, No. 8 (August, 1987), pp. 56-60.

"Recent Exhibitions—Young American Artists," *Arts Magazine*, February 1966, pp. 52-54.

"Santa Fe United States Industrial Indian School," *Ranch and Range*, February 1901, p. 14.

Stacey, Joseph, "Institute of American Indian Arts," *Arizona Highways*, January 1972, pp. 13-14.

"The Old University of New Mexico of Santa Fe," *New Mexico Historical Review*, 8 (December 1956), pp. 201, 206, 210.

The School Arts Magazine, 27, No. 3 (1927); 30, No. 7 (1931); and, 34, No. 7 (1935).

"True West Salutes Chester E. Faris," *True West*, 7 (Jan/Feb. 1960), p. 64.

Waugh, Lynn, "Will Success Spoil Fritz Scholder," *New Mexico Magazine*, May/June 1971, pp. 37-40.

NEWSPAPERS

Santa Fe Weekly New Mexican
    "Santa Fe Indian School," 28 June 1885, p. 4.
    "Worthy Enterprise," 22 April 1886, p. 4.
    "Information From Washington," 8 April 1888, p. 4.

Santa Fe New Mexican
    "Clinton J. Crandall," 23 August 1904, p. 1.
    Ladd, Horatio Oliver, "Founding of Santa Fe Indian Industrial School," 25 September, p.1.
    "Indian Arts Assets," 8 October 1934, p. 4.
    "New Mexico Indians Make History," 11 October 1934, p. 6.
    "Marie Martinez Makes Hit at Indian Exhibit," 12 October 1934, p. 2.
    "Faris Works with Navajos," 18 October 1935, p. 1.
    "French Artist Paul Coze Arranges Show of Indian Watercolors," 27 October 1935, Sec. 2, p. 4.
    "400 Students Register at Indian School," 26 September 1936, p. 6.

"Seymour President of Santa Fe and Albuquerque Schools," 29 September 1936, p. 2.

"Geronima Cruz Interprets Her People," 9 November 1937, p. 2.

"Indian Artists Hold Their Own Exhibit," 3 October 1938, p. 2.

"United Pueblo Agency Builds Building," 16 September 1939, p. 5.

"Accrediting of Indian Schools Urged," 31 August 1941, p. 1.

"Bakos Teaches Art Class," 12 September 1941, p. 3.

"Indian Arts and Crafts Board," 31 September 1941, p. 1.

The New Mexican

Boyce, George A., "Early Days," 8 October 1961, pp. 6-8.

"Indian School Stays Open Year Longer," 6 June 1962, p. 1, cols. 1-3.

"False Mythology on Indian Art Blasted: Truth Cited," 24 June 1962, p. 14, cols. 5-8.

Collins, Jim, "Boyce Shoots Back," 5 August 1962, p. 1, cols. 5-7; p. 5, cols. 3-5.

"Interior Official Defends Art Plans," 5 August 1962, p. 5, cols. 3-4.

"Indians See Opportunity In Institute," 5 August 1962, p. 2, col. 3.

"Chairman Opposes Institute," 6 August 1962, p. 1, col. 6; p. 7, col. 1.

"Don Quixote Rides Again," Editorial, 7 August 1962, p. 4, col. 1.

"Opposition To Art Institute Termed Tragic By Taoseno," 12 August 1962, p. 6, cols. 6-8.

Olive Rush, Letter, 15 August 1962, p. 4, col. 1.

"Institute, Nash Get New Blast," 17 August 1962, p. 1, col. 3; p. 2, col. 6.

"Dorothy Dunn Favors Arts For Indian Institute Here," 28 August 1962, p. 11, cols. 2-3.

"Institute of Indian Arts Opens Oct. 1," 20 September 1962, p. 14.

"Institute Academic Staff, Administration," 4 October 1962, p. 14.

"Indian Art Exhibit"/"Students Exhibit in Capital Show," 17 March 1964, Pasatiempo Section, pp. 1, 8-9.

"Indians Tremendous Hit at White House," 30 March 1965, p. 8, cols. 4-6.

"Indian Arts Receives Jubilant Reception at Capital," 22 April 1965, Sec. A., p. 1, cols., 1-3; p. 2, col. 8.

"New Named Indian Arts Head," 9 August 1967, pp. 1-2.

Windes, Vina, "World Could Profit from Indians' Values," 13 August 1967, Sec. D, p. 2, cols. 1-6.

Waugh, Lynn, "Santa Fe Art," 19 March 1972, Sec. D, p. 2.

Waugh, Lynn, "Portraying the West," 16 July 1972, p. 25.

"Next Year IAIA Middle College," 15 April 1975, Sec. B, p. 1.

"Indian School Control Stressed at Meeting," 9 November 1975, Sec. B, p. 1.

"Retiring IAIA Chief Predicts Better Days," 9 April 1978, Sec. B, p. 1, cols. 3-4.

"The Indian Arts,"28 April 1978, Weekend Section, p. 4.

"SIPI, Other Indian Schools Temporarily Avert Closure," 18 May 1982, Sec. A, p. 2.

IAIA Drum Beats

"Dr. Boyce Retires After Twenty-eight Years in Indian Education," 24 May 1966, pp. 2-3.

The New York Times
Traubman, Howard, "Indians in Santa Fe I," 16 May 1967, p. 42.
Traubman, Howard, "Indians in Santa Fe II, 17 May 1967, p. 55.
IAIA Publication
Smoke Signals (IAIA), 6 April 1965, p. 24.

INTERVIEWS

Pablita Velarde by the American Indian Historical Research Project, University of New Mexico, Albuquerque, New Mexico, 9 February 1972.

Personal Interviews by Author
Carmelita Dunlap, 20 November 1974.
Fritz Scholder, July 1975.
Jose Toledo, September 1975.
Dr. George A. Boyce, Summer/Fall 1976.
Lloyd K. New, 6 May 1977.
Mrs. Oleta Boyce, 15 May 1977.
Carl Tsosie, IAIA, 24 May 1977.
Mrs. Allan Houser, 24 May 1977.
Lloyd New, President, IAIA, and Hank Gobin, Art Director, IAIA, 25 May 1977.
Allan Houser, IAIA, May 1977.
Robert Harcourt, Admission Director, and Jon Wade, President, IAIA, July 1981.
Eugene Fulgenzi, IAIA, July 1981.
Jon Wade, Presdient, IAIA, 14 January 1982.
Robert Harcourt, IAIA, February, 1982.
Charles Poitras, IAIA, February 1982.
Brother Cyprian Luke, President, College of Santa Fe, 12 May 1982.

GOVERNMENT DOCUMENTS

U.S. Department of Interior, Bureau of Indian Affairs, *Report of Superintendent of Indian Schools, 1891* (Washington, D.C.: GPO, 1982), n. pag.
Department of the Interior, *Superintendent of Indian Affairs Annual Report, 1901,* (Washington, D.C.: GPO, 1901), p. 34.
Department of the Interior, *Report of the Secretary of the Interior,* (Washington, D.C.: GPO, 1937), p. 224.
Department of the Interior, *Report of the Secretary of the Interior,* (Washington, D.C.: GPO, 1938), pp. 233-234.
Department of the Interior, *Report of the Secretary of the Interior,* (Washington, D.C.: GPO, 1939), p. 27.
Department of the Interior, *Report of the Secretary of the Interior,* (Washington, D.C.: GPO, 1941), pp. 409-416.

Department of the Interior, *Report of the Secretary of the Interior*, (Washington, D.C.: GPO, 1945), p. 245.

Department of the Interior, *Report of the Secretary of the Interior*, (Washington, D.C.: GPO, 1956), p. 199.

DOCUMENTS HELD IN GEORGE A. BOYCE COLLECTION

Montoya, Geronima, Letter to Martin Vigil, 21 May 1961.

Boyce, George A., "Report to Commissioner of Indian Affairs," 12 December 1961.

Boyce, George A., Letter to Wade Head, Area Director, Gallup Area Office, 16 March 1962.

Carver, John A., Letter to Senator Carl Hayden, 31 July 1962.

Boyce, George A., "Memo for the Record: Some Fundamental Concepts," 14 March 1962.

Boyce, George A., Letter to Robert L. Bennett, Area Director, 12 October 1962.

Boyce, George A., *Progress Report to Gallup Area Director*, 22 October 1962.

Boyce, George A., *Progress Report to Gallup Area Director*, 8 November 1962.

Boyce, George A., Memo to Gallup Area Director, 11 Marcy 1963.

Boyce, George A., Letter to Gallup Area Director, 17 April 1963.

Boyce, George A., Letter to General Superintendent, Navajo Agency, 1 May 1963.

Guice, John, Letter to Gallup Area Director, 14 May 1963.

Boyce, George A., Letter to U.S. Employment Service, 19 April 1963.

Boyce, George A., Letter to Berry's Supermarket, 29 Apirl 1963.

Boyce, George A., Memo to Gallup Area Director, 27 May 1963.

Boyce, A., Memo to Gallup Area Director, 28 May 1963.

Boyce, George A., Letter to Robert L. Bennett, 23 October 1963.

Boyce, George A., Letter to Area Director, 18 December 1963.

Boyce, George A., Memo to Gallup Area Director, 8 January 1964.

Boyce, George A., Letter to Hildegard Thompson, 20 May 1965.

Thompson, Hildegard, Letter to George A. Boyce, n.d. ca. 1965.

Boyce, George A., miscellaneous personal correspondence, 1966.

Students, IAIA, "What I've Gotten out of Being at IAIA," February 1966.

Boyce, George A., private notes, re. "Basic Current Problem of IAIA," 1 March 1966.

Boyce, George A., Memorandum to all employees, re. "Student Art Sales," 1 March 1966.

Boyce, George A., private notes, 4 April 1966.

New, Lloyd K., Letter to George A. Boyce, 14 April 1969.

Boyce, George A., Memorandum to Program Directors, re. "Curricular Policy for Grades 13 and 14, 20 April 1966.

Boyce, George A., private note, n.d., ca. June 1966.

Bennett, Robert L., "Commentary on the Testimony Before the Senate Subcommittee on Indian Education, Februay 2, 1969," n.d., ca. 1969.

U.S. Department of the Interior, Bureau of Indian Affairs, IAIA, "Fact Sheet,"
rev. ed. (Santa Fe: IAIA 1970).

U.S. Department of the Interior, Bureau of Indian Affairs, IAIA, "Purpose
and Philosophy," (Santa Fe: IAIA 1971).

Boyce, George A., Letter to Lynn Waugh, 23 July 1972.

Thompson, Hildegard, Letter to George A. Boyce, July 1972.

Thompson, Morris, Memorandum to all Area Directors, re. "Goals for Indian
Education," March 1974, pp. 1-4.

Thompson, Morris, Memorandum to Acting Area Director, Albuquerque
Area Office, re. "Charter, Administration and Curriculum, IAIA," 3
April 1975.

Boyce, George A., "A Personal Epilogue in Looking Back," 15 June 1976,
unpublished.

Boyce, George A., "Early Days at the Institute of American Indian Arts," pp.
3-4, unpublished.

Boyce, George A., miscellaneous interoffice memos and drafts, ca. 1962-64.

Boyce, George A., private notes, 1964-1966.

GOVERNMENT DOCUMENTS - GENERAL

Hagerman, H. G., "The Indians of the Southwest," Memorandum for the
Secretary of the Interior and Commissioner of Indian Affairs, Santa
Fe, New Mexico, mimeographed, 1 July 1931, p. 31.

Albrecht, Henry J., "Vocational Guidance in the Academic Classroom,"
Indian School Journal of Chilocco Indian Industrial School, January,
1932, p. 14.

Beatty, Willard W., et. al., "Let Us Seek The Quality Market," *Education for
Action: Selected Articles from Indian Education, 1936-1943,* U.S. Department of the Interior, Bureau of Indian Affairs (Washington, D.C.: GPO,
1944), p. 315, 318, 319.

Bureau of Indian Affairs, *Teguayo,* Annual of the Santa Fe Indian School,
(Santa Fe: Santa Fe Indian School, 1962), p. 3.

IAIA, Staff, *The Institute of American Indian Arts, A Basic Statement of Purpose,* original ed. (Santa Fe: IAIA 1962), pp. 1-2, 5-8, 10-11, 12-13, 14-16,
16-17.

Boyce, George A., Letters to Charles J. Rivers, Superintendent, San Carlos
Agency, 12 October 1962.

Warren, Alvin C., "Institute of American Indian Arts to Open at Santa Fe," in
Education for Cross-Cultural Enrichment, ed. Hildegard Thompson,
for U.S. Department of Interior (Washington, D.C.: GPO, 1964), p. 139.

Mizen, Mamie L., *Federal Facilities for Indians,* U.S. Cong., Senate, Committee on Appropriations (November 1964: rpt. Washington, D.C.: GPO,
1965), pp. 3-10.

New, Lloyd K., interoffice memos to Eugene Fulgenzi, 1967-1978. (Held by
Eugene Fulgenzie, Santa Fe).

U.S. Department of the Interior, Bureau of Indian Affairs, Branch of Education, *The Institute of American Indian Arts, Program Memorandum* (n.p.: n.p., 1967), pp. 25, 26, 41, 47-48.

U.S. Department of the Interior, Indian Arts and Crafts Board, *Native American Arts I*, (Washington, D.C.: GPO, 1968).

All Indian Pueblo Council, *A Special Report to the Commissioner of Indian Affairs, Mr. Louis R. Bruce (Albuquerque: n.p., 1970), p.6.*

State of NM, Department of Education, Accreditation Team, The IAIA Program Review (Santa Fe: n.p., 1972), p. 1.

State of NM, Department of Education, Accreditation Team, *The IAIA Program Review,* "Review of Fine Arts Area," by Rollie Heltman, (Santa Fe: n.p., 1972), p. 2.

Tippenconnie, John W., Jr., *The Institute of American Indian Arts Background Information* (Albuquerque: n.p., 1972) p. 8, 8-9, 60.

Bureau of Indian Affairs, Indian Education Resources Center, Albuquerque Office, *Institute of American Indian Arts: Transition Evaluation* (Albuquerque: n.p., 1973), pp. ii-iii, 5-7, 10-14, 21, 38, 119-20, 125.

U.S. Department of the Interior, Bureau of Indian Affairs, IAIA, Special Services Offices, *Guide to Instruction* 1973-73 (Santa Fe: Spec. Svcs. IAIA, 1973), pp. 9-10.

Bureau of Indian Affairs, Indian Education Resources Center, Albuquerque Office, *Institute of American Indian Arts: Transition Evaluation* (Albuquerque: n.p., 1975), pp. 66-67.

U.S. Department of Interior, Bureau of Indian Affairs, *IAIA, Student Handbook 1975-1976,* (Santa Fe: IAIA, 1975), p. 8.

Poitras, Charles, "Institute of American Indian Art," in *BIA College Management Operations Analysis for 1976,* for Office of the Commission of Indian Affairs (Santa Fe: IAIA, 1977), pp. 17, 42-44.

The Native American Council of Regents, *The Future Institute of American Indian Arts and Culture: A Major Multi-Phased National Cultural Advancement Center* (Santa Fe: n.p., 1977), p. 5, 6-8, 72.

New, Lloyd K., Letter to Ms. Jean Ortega, House of Representatives, Committee on Education and Labor, 11 May 1977, pp. 3-4.

Gobin, Hank, Arts Director, Memorandum to Harley Frankel, Deputy Commissioner of Indian Affairs, re. "IAIA's Philosophy and Objections," 18 April 1975, p. 4.

MISCELLANEOUS

Boyce, George A., "Who's Who in the West", 7th ed. (1960).

Moore, James W., Acting Assistant Archivist for the National Archieves, Letter to Senator Pete V. Domenici, on behalf of Winona Garmhausen, 19 August 1981.

Program for the Fourth Annual Scottsdale National Indian Arts Exhibition, 27 February - 7 March 1965.

Warren, Dave, Director, Research and Cultural Studies, IAIA, Letter to Winona Garmhausen, 16 July 1980.

Photo Index

The following photographs, listed with their file numbers, their photographers, and in order of their appearance in the book, are courtesy of the Museum of New Mexico.

The Drummers, photograph by K. Wiest
    courtesty Institute of American Indian Arts, page 93

Third cover photograph and photograph on page 121
    courtesty Winona M. Garmhausen

GENERAL INDEX